CRUSH YOUR KRYPTONITE

HOW TO CONQUER YOUR WEAKNESS AND UNLEASH YOUR SUPERPOWER

NATE HAMBRICK

Copyright © 2022 Nate Hambrick. All rights reserved.

All rights reserved. No part of this publication may be reproduced, distributed, or transmitted in any form or by any means, including photocopying, recording, or other electronic or mechanical methods, without the prior written permission of the publisher, except in the case of brief quotations embodied in critical reviews and certain other noncommercial uses permitted by copyright law.

ISBN Paperback: 979-8-9857010-2-9
ISBN Hardback: 979-8-9857010-0-5
ISBN Audiobook: 979-8-9857010-1-2

DOWNLOAD THE AUDIOBOOK FREE!

To say thanks for buying my book, I would like to give you the audiobook version 100% FREE!

CRUSHYOURKRYPTONITE.COM/AUDIO

TABLE OF CONTENTS

07	INTRODUCTION
11	CHAPTER 1: CRUSH NEGATIVITY
23	CHAPTER 2: MASTER YOUR EFFECTIVENESS
31	CHAPTER 3: CRUSH PERPETUAL NOISE
41	CHAPTER 4: CRUSH YOUR ENTITLEMENT
53	CHAPTER 5: MASTER YOUR PRIORITIES AND POTENTIAL
75	CHAPTER 6: CRUSH YOUR PROCRASTINATION
93	CHAPTER 7: MASTER YOUR FRIENDSHIPS
103	CHAPTER 8: YOUR SUPERPOWER'S KRYPTONITE
111	CHAPTER 9: HOW WILL YOU CRUSH YOUR KRYPTONITE?
121	BOOKS TO READ FOR FURTHER DEVELOPMENT

INTRODUCTION

Everyone is born into this world a hero destined for greatness. No villain is our match, no prize beyond our reach. Life is a wonderful place filled with endless opportunities. The challenge before us is that we all also have Kryptonites—weaknesses that neutralize our superpowers and hold us back from what we are destined to become. Either you will crush your Kryptonite, or it will eventually crush you. It's easy to ignore, most of the time. Usually, it is far enough away that you can pretend it's not slowly killing you. Still, you feel your Kryptonite's effect and know you should deal with it.

You can crush it at any time, whether the beginning, middle, or end of your life. The question is, will you?

Some subdue their Kryptonite immediately so they can peacefully enjoy the rest of their lives, but most avoid it for as long as they can. Avoiding it only weakens them, leaving them perpetually ineffective. It's not long before what once was a perfect dreamland of opportunity turns into a dull life of mediocrity.

We will all have to face many battles in this life. We can't stop them from coming, but we can—to a significant degree—improve our ability to prevail. Each battle differs, but the principles for winning them remain consistent: recognize your Kryptonite, and then crush it.

Hi, I'm Nate Hambrick and I'm the author of this book. I won't pretend to have a perfect life, and I won't pretend to have everything figured out, but I do live by certain principles that have made me an extremely effective person. I've broken records for every single company I've worked for, I've written and recorded eight commercially distributed music albums, and, more importantly, I've been able to help lots of people overcome obstacles and achieve big goals through the principles I am about to share.

Everyone has something in them that has held them back from their true potential, so I wrote this book to help you deal with it. The strategies in this book aren't just for the young and hungry business professionals, but for the stay-at-home moms, the retail workers, and anyone else who is tired of getting in their own way—whether that's through procrastination, perfectionism, apathy, negativity, or something else. Mediocrity is comfortable and safe, but the extraordinary lives we could lead if we addressed our flaws is worth the pain of facing them.

Before we begin, I want to clarify that this book is not about hypotheticals or intellectual discourse for the sake of sounding wise while doing nothing. It's about taking massive action and getting the most out of life. It's also rather blunt, and that's because I think you may need to hear some of these things candidly if you want to overcome your weaknesses and live your best life.

Each of the following chapters addresses Kryptonites you may face and ways you can crush them and move on. I've included action steps at the end of each chapter that will help you get the most out of this book. If I've done my job right, by the end of this book, you will know exactly how to take action in your life and *Crush Your Kryptonite*.

CHAPTER ONE

CRUSH NEGATIVITY

I first acknowledged that negativity was a Kryptonite of mine my senior year in college, but let me tell you a bit more of my story, first.

My journey of indoctrination into the self-help world began when a friend convinced me to join an internship, selling children's books door-to-door. For twelve weeks, every facet of our lives was extreme. We greeted the day at 5:59 a.m. to remind ourselves that normal people wake up at 6:00 a.m. Within seconds of the alarm's chirp, we would hit the floor for fifty push-ups and plunge ourselves into frigidly cold Michigan showers to wake ourselves up quickly. We even dreamed up "Coldarus," a fictional Greek god of cold showers, and we communed with his icy waters daily. We would pack our bags and leave the crash pad by 6:15 a.m. every morning and wouldn't return until around 10 p.m., Monday through Saturday. Including Sunday training sessions, we worked one hundred and fifteen hours a week, the bulk of which was cold calling door-to-door. Cell phones were banned to avoid distractions, and walking was frowned upon. Everything centered around a singular task: maximizing book sales.

This culture was a new beginning for me. I used to be surrounded by "average" and "good enough," and I rarely stumbled across anyone whose dreams compelled them to sacrifice everything to obtain them. But these crazy book-slingers were different. They genuinely believed they were 100 percent in control of their attitude and effort and were, therefore, 100 percent in control of their destiny. This was the kind of environment where legends are born. Their standards were high, and their heroes were those who denied themselves the most comfort in the name of overcoming adversity. Their universe revolved around denying self in order to sell as many books as possible, and they inundated us with stories to promote that. One man fell into a sewage drain and continued selling door-to-door with a smile on his face and sewer water on his clothes. He could have quickly gone home to change, but the moral of the story is that there is no excuse for quitting, even for a moment. Another man wrecked his car but sold books while riding a bicycle, even though he was in the country where it was miles between houses. The more ridiculous the situation, the more excitement it generated. We aspired to be like these heroes, full of grit, determination, and an insatiable desire to never give up in the face of adversity.

"I am in control" was their mantra and North Star. I dove in headfirst and drank the Kool-Aid from day one. Phrases like "Just be yourself" or "You do you" were utterly unacceptable here. Entertaining even the most legitimate roadblocks to success were instantly disregarded as excuses for mediocrity. Despite the hardship, this was a wonderful time for me, and the best was yet to come.

Door-to-door sales was the first place I truly understood the importance of crushing negativity with affirmations and positive self-talk, because

I was able to see its effects daily. Until this point, the only frame of reference I had for affirmations was my eccentric grandmother popping around the corner saying, "If you believe it, you can achieve it!" It sounded like a load of rubbish at the time, but as I came to learn, due to the nature of door-to-door sales in the 21st century, affirmations were vital to our success.

From a physiological standpoint, our brains are hellbent on negativity, especially in extreme conditions. To combat this, we trained ourselves to talk positively, out loud, all day long, like a crazy person. The concept is simple: if you're saying positive things constantly, your brain can't poison itself with negativity. I can tell you—from a decade of experience—that positive self-talk will help you if you find yourself caught in a negative mental spiral.

In that environment, verbal affirmations were an absolute lifesaver. We couldn't afford to let our brains be negative—or even neutral, for that matter. We needed to proactively coerce our brains into choosing joy, regardless of external factors.

I still use self-talk when I'm in a lull or have a slight chance of going negative. Choosing to be positive has made all the difference. I am responsible for my attitude. (By the way, shameless plug for Og Mandino's book, *The Greatest Salesman in the World*. Contrary to its name, it has very little to do with sales. It's a collection of powerful affirmations to read daily, and it's a great way to speak life-giving truths to yourself.)

Positive self-talk saved my career when I was in business-to-business financial services. Fear of the unknown is one of the most common challenges in direct sales. I've been in thousands of businesses in every industry under the sun, and each one was a different experience. I never knew whom I would meet or how it would go. Sometimes it was smooth sailing, and I would walk out laughing with the owner. Other times, I would meet people who were having a rough go at it long before I got there. Negative interactions and explosive rejection are "agent killers" that quickly destroy sales careers. The ones who last are the ones who aggressively wage war on their own negative thoughts and don't let fear of the unknown crush them.

At one time, I had been selling insurance for three months, but the only success I had was in the first couple of weeks. Rejection set in soon afterward. I was in my head, and I was falling victim to the "the car trap." The car trap would start as five to ten minutes of preparation, sitting in my car, for the next interaction. Before I knew it, I was spending an hour in my car before each interaction—in my head, trapped in an endless cycle of negativity.

"This is hard. What if the next person hates me?"
"What if they think I'm scamming them?"
"What if they're busy, and I'll blow my chance of a good introduction because I didn't come at the right time?'
"What is the right time?"
"What if I'm wasting their time?"
"What if *I* am a waste of time?"

I was allowing the mental funk to consume me, and it was decimating my confidence (and my income.)

To combat this, I used the principles I learned in door-to-door sales as a college student, and I crushed my Kryptonite. I took the negativity that was killing me, and I brutally killed it. Like in *The Godfather*, I gave myself "an offer [I] couldn't refuse." The offer I gave myself was to talk out loud every second of the day, and if I ever stayed in my car for more than ten minutes, I would owe my friend Josh $500 per infraction. As you can imagine, this put an end to all of the sitting-in-my-car nonsense. This deal I made with myself helped my brain make the connection of just how expensive my negativity was, which helped me neutralize it almost instantly.

Two days later, I was battling insecurity and—if I'm being honest—I really wanted to give up. Sitting in my car past the ten-minute mark was tempting, but I forced myself out. Even though I felt nervous and unprepared, I went into a small coffee shop and talked to the owner, who ended up being incredible.

We instantly hit it off, and as we spoke, I learned that he ran the business with his wife. Because I wanted to pitch him, I asked him to bring his wife out so I could show them what I was doing for some of their friends. The mood shifted when his ill-tempered wife appeared and started yelling at me for no apparent reason. I was surprised, and he was embarrassed because she was disturbing the peace in their quiet little coffee shop.

But just as things were going wrong, the positive self-talk and momentum I had built that day paid off. Because I hadn't allowed myself to get in my head, I was able to handle it calmly. I took a few steps back, raised my hands, and super lightheartedly laughed.

"Whoa," I said, "I'm only here because your friends asked me to catch up with you." After an awkwardly long pause, I continued, "Would it be okay if I gave you a quick look at what we're doing for your friends, ____ and ____?"

Long story short, I walked out of there fifteen minutes later with $1,000 in revenue and a giant smile on my face. I owed all of that to the fact I crushed my Kryptonite of negativity. The long-term effects are still paying me dividends to this day—both figuratively and literally, because I'm still collecting renewal income from that transaction six years later. That victory led to closing deals with three large police departments that week, and eventually closing deals with companies like Anytime Fitness, Skechers, Holiday Inn, BBVA Compass, O'Reillys, Autozone, Subway, Taco Bell, Wendy's, Sonic, Sherwin-Williams, Verizon, Sprint, and hundreds more.

I kept that standard during several parts of my career. Over this course of time, I failed "the car trap" three times, and paid three friends $500 each because of my weakness. Committing to crushing my negativity was expensive—$1,500, to be precise. But the price of being average was significantly more costly.

I think about it this way: if I hadn't started conquering negativity and making these uncommon choices, then I wouldn't have quadrupled my income, I wouldn't have the business relationships I have, and I definitely wouldn't be making the same level of impact. And that's the lesson. *Not* crushing whatever is holding you back comes at an unfathomable opportunity cost, but most of us never realize what we're missing out on. It's a treasure we never knew we gave up.

So the question is, how do you identify and crush negativity when it is crippling you? After all, the people around you are most likely engaging with negativity, so why should you be any different? I'll tell you why. Because you *are* different. I don't think it's an accident you picked up a book called *Crush Your Kryptonite*. You most likely recognize that you want more out of life, so now it's time to put in the hard work of changing your default suppositions and behaviors.

Developing good self-talk is just like developing any other habit. It takes work to replace a poor habit with a more favorable one. I recommend putting reminders in the most common places where you live and work to help you with this. I used to tape note cards that said, "Are you talking out loud?" to the steering wheel of my car and above the light switches in my house. This has proven to be an effective way to remind me that I'm responsible for change in my life.

Life is hard, and it will continue to bombard you with an onslaught of difficulties until the day you die, so focus on the *positive* areas of your life or your hardship will consume you. Positive self-talk is one of the many tactics you can employ to crush negativity so it doesn't crush you.

At the time of this writing, the world is still going through the COVID-19 pandemic. It's sad to see how many of my old friends spend more time complaining about how hard life is than they spend improving their circumstances. Yes, life is hard. It's been that way since the beginning of time, but blaming your circumstances won't solve the issue. This learned helplessness we've adopted is just as dangerous as the virus itself. Victimhood is a losing strategy for all areas of life. It makes us passive and allows us to avoid taking responsibility for the things we can influence.

On the flip side, there is always a solution when we admit our part of the problem. When the virus first shut the world down, there was more opportunity than I had ever seen, but no one seemed to recognize it. I wasn't sure if my sales job would survive this, so I pivoted and did fast-food and grocery delivery in my spare time. I was not giving in to negativity around me. I was taking responsibility for the things I could influence and control, and taking advantage of the new world of opportunity.

I made a killing doing mundane activities because everyone else was terrified they would die. More importantly, I had a lot of fun. It felt like the world had gone to sleep. Traffic was better than ever, and I enjoyed my work a lot because I chose to see it as a once-in-a-lifetime chance to get ahead. I remember dropping food off at people's homes and hearing timid voices calling back, "be safe out there." I appreciated their genuine concern, but I was chuckling on the inside. I was not a victim. I was cheerful as ever, taking advantage of every new opportunity that presented itself.

And I wasn't alone. According to the Institute for Policy Studies, fifty-six people made the leap from millionaire status to billionaire status between mid-March and Dec. 22, 2020.[1] The people who were already winning took advantage of the opportunities created by the fearful majority and climbed to new heights of success. They did that because that's what winners do. They win. When life is easy, they're figuring out new ways to improve themselves and create value for others. When life is challenging, they pivot and continue figuring out new ways to

---

[1] Martha C. White, "Wall Street Minted 56 New Billionaires Since the Pandemic Began — But Many Families are Left Behind," *NBC News*, Dec 30, 2020, https://www.nbcnews.com/business/business-news/wall-street-s-best-year-ever-why-pandemic-has-been-n1252512.

improve themselves and create value for others. Nothing changes except the circumstances they're dealing with.

Fear is a wonderful instinct that warns us of danger, but it will rob you of a wonderful life if you succumb to it. So then, how do you crush fear while still addressing the issue? How can you benefit from it without giving into it?

Fear is useful when it is acting as a warning sign—it tells me that if I walk too close to a cliff, I might fall off and die. Fear becomes counterproductive if (and when) it keeps me from hiking at all because of that possibility of falling. The difference is whether you choose to face your fear head-on, or retreat because of it.

Crushing your negativity frees you and enables you to get more out of life. This is one of the first steps toward unlocking your superpower. Continue on to discover more insights on how to increase your effectiveness.

ACTION STEPS

WHAT IS YOUR BIGGEST KRYPTONITE?

_____
_____
_____
_____
_____
_____
_____

WHAT IS YOUR GAME PLAN TO CRUSH IT?

_____
_____
_____
_____
_____
_____
_____

> I'd rather be optimistic and wrong than pessimistic and right.
>
> – **ELON MUSK**

CHAPTER TWO

MASTER YOUR EFFECTIVENESS

In the last chapter, we talked about the importance of crushing negativity, because it's one of the biggest Kryptonites that will keep you from your true potential. But positivity alone won't help you achieve meaningful goals. You also need to be effective.

The two key components to becoming an effective person are knowing your *why* (in other words, your goal or purpose—knowing "why" you are doing this) and building a plan to get there. Tony Robbins is famously quoted for stating, "People are not lazy. They simply have impotent goals—that is, goals that do not inspire them." I have learned the hard way that when I don't know *why* I'm doing something or how to get there, I lose focus and end up nowhere. In the words of my buddy, Dillon, the last words we say before we quit are, "Well, why the F*** am I doing this?" Finding our *why* makes aligning our actions with our ambitions much more effortless.

You're not lazy. You just might not know where you're headed or *why* you should get there. Finding your reason for doing any action is essential to its success. For example, if you set a fitness goal and don't know your *why*, it's unlikely you'll get there. To make that goal more inspiring, you must ask yourself, "*Why* do I want to be fit?"

Before becoming the powerlifting champion in college, I knew I wanted to be muscular. Still, that goal of "becoming muscular," in and of itself, is uninspiring and would not have given me the courage to wake up early for years on end, lifting weights that could easily break me in two. Impotent goals are like unrealistic New Year's resolutions; gone by February and utterly worthless.

The most effective way to set goals is to tie them to your emotional being. When I set a fitness goal, I set it for the pinnacle of fitness. I'm talking bodybuilder magazine, "super unattainable," six-pack abs, 5 percent body fat type of fit. I wanted to achieve something truly impressive.

Now the question is, *why* did I want that? Well, I wanted that to compensate for my lack of stature. I'm just shy of five-eight, so although I'm less than two inches short of the national average, I wanted to be in the top 1 percent of fitness because of the way it would make me feel and the way it would make me look. Some of my friends asked me, "Nate, isn't that kind of unnecessary?" Of course, it's unnecessary, but I wanted it, so I went for it. I was going to be the best-looking dude at the pool party. At *any* pool party.

Adding to that deep purpose, at the time, I was still searching for the woman of my dreams. I used that deep-seated emotion as fuel for my activities. Hitting my goal was a piece of cake because my whole being was involved in its pursuit. When I lifted weights, I wasn't just lifting weights; I was creating the body of my dreams, attracting my future wife, getting noticed by the best employers, and elevating my social prowess. My goal reverberated throughout my whole being and was significantly more inspiring than, "I'm going to the gym so I can be healthy." If you set a target, make sure you dig into your *why* until it lights a fire under you or brings a smile to your face. If it doesn't, you're probably not setting the right goal.

The same principle applies everywhere. If you set a goal to double your income just because you like money, that would be a hollow and meaningless goal. But if you ask yourself *why* you want to double your income, that may lead you to deeper motivation. Is it so you can spend more time with your family? Is it so your wife can travel the world like she's wanted to since she was a little girl? Is it so you can purchase cash-flow-producing assets so you won't be a lifelong wage slave? Is it so you can help more people and have an impact?

Okay. Why do you want that? Keep following that up with another *why* until it's gone as far as it can go. You will have a much better chance of getting where you want to go when you do that.

For me, increasing my income is important but not for the typical reasons. My *why* is threefold. First off, I don't want to work for every dollar I make and stress over it for the rest of my life. Second, I want to build an endowment fund for underpaid pastors and missionaries abroad. I think it's a tragedy that our most servant-hearted, loving, and selfless leaders are barely scraping by, and I want to change that. And third, I want to know that I'm bringing a ton of value to people. It's not about the money. It's about what the money says; that I'm worth every penny.

When I think about the relationship I want with my kids and the peace and rest that comes from not focusing on bills, I am truly inspired to do hard things. I follow my *why* until I'm a little embarrassed by the vulnerable answer it produces.

Now that you understand how to uncover your *why*, it's time to develop your plan to get there.

Step 1. Define your goals.
Step 2. Develop clear metrics for how you will get there.
Step 3. Review your goals daily.

When I open my laptop every morning, the first web page I see is my identity statement and goals for the month. Each goal has a plan in place for how I'm getting there and the weekly metrics I need to achieve it. I also include my fitness, marriage, and other personal goals, which I review every morning. I ensure their achievement by reminding myself *why* my goals matter and how I'm getting there. Not only does this steer me toward the right activities, but it also gives me strength when I need it. The more consistent I am at putting my dreams and desires in front of myself, the easier it is to overcome the challenges life will send me.

There's no way around it—life involves constant sacrifice. Saying "yes" to one thing means saying "no" to another. Life's biggest winners constantly give up short-term desires for their long-term dreams.

Prioritize your dreams and eliminate any hindrances.

I have learned throughout my career that multitasking is ineffective, and extreme single-tasking produces better results. As far as I can tell, multitasking is a myth. A much more effective method is to list your priorities in a row and then knock them out, one at a time. Don't try to do two things at once. It's not helpful. I am laser-focused on the most important tasks when I'm working, and I procrastinate everything else until they're done. Typically speaking, one or two tasks drive 80 percent of my results. That's where I'm going to focus all my efforts. If I treat all tasks as equal, I will waste my time filling my stapler, cleaning my desk, and organizing files, but I won't get any real results.

Do you see what I'm getting at? Finding your *why* and solidifying your *how* empowers you to distinguish the difference between worthwhile aspirations and beautiful distractions. This is the path toward effectiveness.

ACTION STEPS

CREATE A VISION STATEMENT FOR YOUR LIFE

Year-long goals:

Monthly goals:

Jan

Feb

Mar

Apr

May

Jun

Jul

Aug

Sep

Oct

Nov

Dec

Weekly Metrics: ....
....

Your emotional Why for each item listed above: ....
....

Review your vision statement every morning and enjoy the extra ground you'll be covering due to your extraordinary and uncommon focus.

CHAPTER THREE

CRUSH PERPETUAL NOISE

When I was an insurance agent, I had an appointment in a government-subsidized apartment. As I entered their home, the walls of their apartment were reverberating the sounds of an obnoxious, cheap television in the corner. When I asked the owners if they could mute it while we talked, one of them piped up and said, "I'm not sure where the remote is. We lost it a couple years ago."

I mistakenly thought they meant that we would have to adjust it manually, so I walked over to the TV and responded, "Oh, that's okay, we can just turn it off then."

"I don't think the TV has buttons on it," they responded.

In shock, I turned around and asked, "Do you mean to tell me you've been sleeping with the television on for two years straight?"

"Yep!" they responded, laughing as they moved the dusty furniture to pull the power cord from the wall.

It's no wonder their lives were in visible disarray. Who could possibly think straight in that environment? I can't imagine getting anything productive done after years of consistent noise.

On a subconscious level, I believe they were endlessly distracting themselves to drown out the overwhelming sadness of their lives. There's chaos within all of us, and sometimes it's easier to ignore heartbreak and tragedy than it is to face it. Living with your Kryptonite is easier than crushing it.

As I walked away from their apartment, I asked myself, "Nate, are there any ways (as small as they might be) in which you have been acting like them?"

I realized I was no different. I consistently pull out my phone to avoid social awkwardness in public settings. I incessantly check my texts and emails, even when I clearly don't need to. By speeding up and filling every lull with perpetual noise, I avoid the deafening silence of my shortcomings and failures. But it's a hamster wheel I can't outrun. Avoiding my faults and failures only allows them to continue impacting me negatively.

That interaction was a wake-up call for me. For the previous four years, I hadn't embraced the silence long enough to assess my trajectory. Winning seemed to be more important than taking a stroll through my wandering thoughts. Any time my mind told me to quit, give up, or change course, I silenced it with positivity and pressed on. Eventually, I just couldn't keep it up, and I was finally willing to pause long enough to question my life.

And so, that's what I did. I questioned everything. With no warning to my friends or family, I took the week off, sat alone in the woods, and let my thoughts wander to wherever they wanted to take me. "Am I proud of what I'm doing? Am I proud of who I am and how I treat people? Am I proud of what I do for a living?"

As far as my career was concerned, the answer was no. I was not proud. Sure, there was plenty of glitz and glam I could focus on, but that didn't negate the bucket full of crap sitting in the corner. The stench was still there, and I knew it. Reality hit me with full force. I shouldn't keep doing this. There were certain uncontrollable facets of the insurance business I was running, making it impossible for me to be both successful and fully live up to my standard of integrity. I had told myself I was giving people a fantastic opportunity and believing in them when no one else would, but I soon realized this was a creative way of relying on grossly under-qualified and under-emotionally prepared novices to take on a brutal, commission-based sales job. Truthfully, I was giving them an amazing opportunity—I was given the same opportunity—but the difference was that it was an incredible gig for a hungry, self-motivated, and highly disciplined person like me. It was *not* a good fit for someone who could barely keep an ordinary job in the first place. My people were failing left and right, and nothing in my power could make them succeed.

Eventually, I realized I was the problem. The perpetual noise in my life had allowed me to ignore that act for far longer than I should have. It was time to deal with the issue and find a new path forward. Even though I had planned on staying at this insurance agency until retirement, that week of forest meditation made me realize that even if I made all the money in the world, I still wouldn't be happy if I wasn't living up to my moral code. So I quit my job, and I am so much happier today for it.

This balance between self-help wisdom and inner reflection has been so valuable in my life, as it has kept me on the straight and narrow. As a sales rep, most of my time needs to be spent aggressively pursuing my work with positivity, but, I went wrong by allowing a positive tool to turn into perpetual noise, which drowned everything else out. I had let the noise of crushing my Kryptonites of negativity and inefficiency drown out my angst within, which was trying to tell me to modify my targets and adjust my trajectory. If I had a little more space to realize this, I would have saved a couple of years of my life and been much further along the path to my *real* goals.

This is a neglected piece of the puzzle with most of the self-help books and inspirational speakers I follow. I could easily devote myself toward a few impactful goals, which is good, but I could also become so devoted to them that I forgot to evaluate and adjust as I go. As beneficial as self-talk is, I have equally benefited from sitting alone in the woods—without my phone—and asking myself, "Am I proud of what I'm doing? Am I proud of the person I'm becoming? Am I proud of how I treat people? In what ways am I helping people, and in what ways am I hurting people?"

Busyness is a convenient way to numb the pain inside of us. Social media, music, television, and the internet are some of the most convenient ways we silence ourselves. Are you feeling bad about yourself? Here are twenty TV shows where idiots make horrifically stupid choices to make you feel better about yourself. Are you creatively avoiding a difficult task? Here is an endless supply of noise for the low price of $7.99 a month.

We need space to let our brains tell us what's happening in our hearts. Perpetual noise is a bad habit for many, but it's most noticeable in lower-income households, where it's not uncommon to see multiple TVs or radios on simultaneously. The chaos is baffling. That extreme case of perpetual noise was blatantly obvious, and it helped me understand the root issue within myself—the quieter, but still noisy subtleties of my own self-sabotage.

It kills me to watch how perpetual noise kills people's drive and keeps them poor in mind, spirit, and body. It's unfortunate. The most tragic part is, they're not as sad about it as I am, because they're medicating their sadness with noise so they don't have to face its disastrous impact. In their distracted state, they can't see the devastatingly high opportunity cost of not taking responsibility for the outcome of their lives. That blindness frequently leads to blame-shifting. It's not *my* fault my life isn't going anywhere. It's the government's fault. It's society's fault. I might not even know whose fault it is, but it is someone else's fault.

Perpetual noise is a numbing agent that allows underlying issues to remain unaddressed. If you broke your arm, anesthesia would make the experience much more bearable. This is a good thing. But continuing to indefinitely numb the pain without addressing what's causing the pain— your broken arm—would be foolish. The same thing applies to our lives. We feel an emptiness within, so we fill our time with fun things.

This temporarily makes us happy, so it's easy to convince ourselves it's positive. But fun activities don't actually improve us, so we remain relatively stagnant. We hinder our progress by accepting our lives as is, instead of looking for new ways to grow.

I'd go as far as to say that perpetual noise is one of the most common Kryptonites we face. Here's why you should pay attention to this: let's say every couple of days, life gives you one small opportunity to either rise above and improve yourself or remain stagnant. Examples of this might be a brief interaction with a stranger, or a lull in your day. At face value, they might not seem like opportunities, but what if the brief interaction with a stranger ends up being a connection that lands you your next job or investment opportunity? What if you spent that lull in your day to solidify your dreams so you could pursue them with greater clarity? These moments might only be a 1 percent course correction, but one slight adjustment compounded every few days for the next ten years will land you in a whole new world of opportunity. While the world around you is begging for distractions to unwind and entertain themselves, you can systematically improve yourself, so when life's biggest opportunities come knocking on your door, you're the most prepared and qualified to take them on.

Now that we've established noise as a serious issue, how do you identify and crush perpetual noise? After all, ironically, it's a *silent* killer. It probably isn't even on your radar; you could easily suffer from it your entire life and never acknowledge its presence.

The simple revelation I've come to is that you need to pause. Whether it's getting alone in the woods or just taking one minute right now, you need to pause. Get rid of your phone, get rid of your distractions, and let your mind guide you where it pleases. This is your life. Are you who you want to be?

ACTION STEPS

THINK THROUGH THE FOLLOWING QUESTIONS:

What two distractions should I cut from my life?

Am I proud of my actions, attitudes, and results in my:

Family life?:

Work-life?:

Spiritual life?:

"

Never let the noise
of the world overpower
the stillness of your soul.

– AUTHOR UNKNOWN

CHAPTER FOUR

CRUSH YOUR ENTITLEMENT

The belief that "society owes me" is quite common. This lie shows up everywhere, and in differing forms of entitlement. "Everyone deserves free healthcare." "Everyone deserves free education." "Tax the rich." I've even seen memes advocating we seize billionaire's assets to pay off student loans. At first, I assumed people were just venting and didn't actually believe these ridiculous notions. Then I spent time on Facebook during an election, and I was appalled by the things people believe and are bold enough to post. The underlying assumption is that life should be easy for us and that people should adapt to fill our needs for us. This is especially true regarding jobs, income, and status.

My question is, why? Why do we believe we are owed anything? We live in one of the most prosperous generations in the history of the world. We have access to the entire planet via the internet, which means that the only reason we can't get what we want is ourselves.

In part, I can understand the belief that "If I work hard, I deserve a living wage." That sounds fair, but if you're working hard at making mud pies in your backyard, you're not adding value to anyone's life. We get paid to solve problems, not just to work hard. How did we get to a place where we believe that a complete stranger owes us anything? Surely, we wouldn't believe that if the roles were reversed. If a stranger demanded you pay their bills, you'd be shocked and would send them packing. So, why do we fall for the idealistic society where everything is given to us?

Newsflash: life is hard. As much as we all would selfishly love to live in a supportive utopia where we are the center of the universe, that's just not how life is.

The cruelties of life are not entirely pointless. We go through them for a reason. They build character and help us understand that our choices have consequences, both negatively and positively. The kid that gets knocked down a thousand times and still gets up again is the one who has the most fulfilling life in the end. If you think an easy life will make you happy, you're wrong. Rare is the lottery winner who ends up happier and more fulfilled because of it. Because they didn't put themselves through the refinement that is typically required to amass that level of fortune, they typically falter. Nothing inside them changed when they won, so the illness within will continue to fester—except now, they can do whatever they want, opening new opportunities to inflict havoc on themselves and society. That's why we must crush the lie that society owes us anything. Not only is it not true, but it also wouldn't serve us even if it were true.

Once you accept that the outcome of your life rests solely in your hands, you can regain the control you gave up by playing a passive role. If you want to get more, do more and help more. It's that simple. Go find someone and fix their problems. The bigger the problem, the bigger the payday. The harder the skill set required, the more potential there is for you to thrive. The more people you help, the more times you'll be paid. That's why I'm not entitled to anything. If I'm helping people, I can help myself. But if I'm selfish and spend more time complaining than I spend developing a useful skill, no one will help me in return.

That's one of the main reasons I'm in sales. It's a way for me to solve thousands of people's problems in a short period of time. The problem I solve for the client is getting them the help they need, and the problem I solve for the company is revenue. I work for a fantastic company. They have great products and great people, but they don't have a business without clients and revenue. When I first got into sales, I was bringing in chump change. Then, I started bringing in hundreds of thousands of dollars. I'm currently responsible for bringing in 1.5 million a year, and it'll be tens of millions one day. The bigger the problem I solve, the better I'm compensated for it.

When I hire a car mechanic, I'm paying him to solve my problem. The bigger the problem, the more I'll pay him. One time, I had a broken windshield. I found a guy online who would drive to my house and swap out the window in my driveway. It was awesome. Not only was he solving my windshield issue, but he was also solving my time issue. I didn't want to waste three hours waiting in a repair shop. Because he came to me, I guarded my revenue-generating time, which paid for the windshield he was fixing. Because he was willing to come to me, I gave him the business over someone else. It was a win-win.

Small problems pay well, too, but you need to do more of them to make up for the difference. For example, if you're in retail, you solve simple problems like food and clothing, so if you want more, you will need to solve problems faster. If you're making a dollar per problem solved, well then, figure out how to solve that problem for 100,000 people. Amazon didn't make it big by solving big problems but by solving billions of small problems. That's the fundamental principle of entrepreneurship: find a problem, then figure out how to solve it for less than it would cost the other person to solve.

I know people who are so stressed they can't think straight. Instead of focusing on the problem, they spend all their time worrying and complaining about it. They need to crush those fears and aggressively develop the people skills and problem-solving skills they'll need to get out of it. That's why I love companies like Shipt, Instacart, and Uber. They've lowered the barrier to entry by opening up a whole new world of instant problem-solving opportunities at a moment's notice.

Oh, you randomly had your Friday night open up? Great, do a couple of grocery runs, take a stranger to the airport, get some drunk party people home safely. Solve somebody's problems and solve your own.

There are always inevitable excuses to these kinds of jobs. "But it's not safe to have a stranger in my car." "But I'm looking for something that's in my field." "But my wife and I want to spend time together in the evenings."

Well then, spend time doing grocery runs together. If you're broke enough to complain, you're broke enough to work your way out of the hole you dug. Whatever the excuse, figure it out—or have fun being

Eeyore the rest of your life. Either way, crush your *entitlement* and don't blame society for your choices.

The "Just Be Yourself" Excuse

There are many examples where "just be yourself" is used positively. I am not negating any of these. Instead, I am trying to explain how this cute phrase has turned into a Kryptonite for mediocrity and excuses.

It's like if a second grader were to tell his mom, "Hey, Mom, I'm not going to school anymore because it's just not my thing. Some people were made for school, but I'm made for hanging around the house and playing games."

No loving parent would give in to that excuse. If they did, they would be putting their child's future in jeopardy. However, as adults, we say the same kinds of things all the time. "Oh, that's just not my thing. I wish I could get that high-paying job, but I'm just not wired for that." Newsflash: you're not naturally wired for brushing your teeth, eating healthy, treating others well, or any number of positive societal traits. Growing up, if it were up to you, you would eat Cap'n Crunch and ice cream every day, never brush your teeth, and treat others as objects to be abused. If your parents didn't discipline you consistently throughout childhood and force you to have basic healthy habits, you would be a decrepit disaster by now. Thank God someone pushed back on your temporal and selfish desires when you were young.

Now you're all grown up and have learned how to be an upstanding citizen with a positive impact on society. That's great, but the problem is now *you* have to take on the role of your parents and coerce yourself toward the things that build you up—and away from the things that kill you. That's more challenging because, just as when you were a child, it was easy to ignore the negative implications of your poor habits. If you're not careful, you will end up killing yourself slowly with no one to intervene on your behalf.

"I'm just being myself" is used for all manners of justification for behaviors that should probably be addressed. This phrase is destructive because it shuts down conversation. If someone in a group of friends defensively says, "Stop judging me, I'm just being myself," the whole group will instantly step back for fear of getting their head bit off. This allows the person with the destructive behavior to continue destroying themselves.

The problem is, there are so many positive arguments for "just be yourself," but most of them are wishful thinking and completely hypothetical. If you want to know if something is true, look at the results of the people who follow that advice. Are the people at the top saying, *just be yourself*? Heck no. The only exception I can think of is celebrities pandering to their fans, but that's about it. This cute saying has more negative side effects than positive ones.

I know people who passed on their dream job because they wouldn't cut their hair or change how they dressed. "Just be yourself" is an expensive ideology. Changing a society of millions of people is much harder than just changing yourself, so why fight it? If transforming yourself in small ways like hair or dress is the extent of "not being true to yourself," I say, do it. That's not giving up on yourself; that's called growth. Embrace the change.

When I started in door-to-door sales, it only took me a couple weeks of failing to realize I needed to be less intimidating to strangers when I knocked on their door. Even though I had never worn pastel shorts and tight polos in my life, I decided to dress like a frat kid to suit the people I was serving. Nobody, not even the single mother, fears the frat-daddy. My ability to adapt translated into more dollars in my pocket, more people helped, and more relationships built. I may not have been being entirely "myself," but I have no regrets about that.

When I was a business-to-business sales trainer, I helped a marine who had recently retired from the service. He had been a very successful military commander, and he embodied every marine stereotype. He would enter businesses with his sunglasses on, looking like a killer, and then wonder why no one wanted to speak with him. No matter how much I told him to smile and leave the sunglasses in the car, he would say, "My sunglasses are a part of me." Not surprisingly, he and his sunglasses didn't last very long. And for what? So he could wear shades indoors? Come on, man, that's ridiculous. He intimidated everyone but expected them to adapt instead of changing himself. This was a losing strategy.

So what's the alternative? Give up on everything that makes you, you?

No, of course not. With every circumstance, ask yourself if the behavior in question is keeping you from where you want to be. If it is, then give it up. Just like you would never give into a child's destructive behaviors simply because they claimed they were "being themselves," don't give in to the same ridiculous excuses for yourself. If there's a part of you that doesn't serve you, get rid of it and move on. Your future self will thank you.

Let me give you a third example. This one is a little touchier, so my apologies in advance. I have a friend who is an ethnic minority, and she protested her white boss asking her not to wear dreadlocks and a bandana in front of customers. She was furious. On some level, I think this is a reasonable thing to protest. I would be offended, too, if I was told to change my hair so people would like me more. Although I empathize with her, what is she going to do? Change stereotypes for millions of people? She didn't want to dress like a professional, so why should she expect to be paid like one? The lie lurking in the shadows here is, "people should accept me as I am." Although this would be absolutely wonderful, it's not based on reality. If you want to succeed in life, either move to a place where society champions you exactly as you are, or adapt to your surroundings. I would argue that the latter is a much easier strategy, and I would also say that, in a way, it's your way of loving the people around you. The alternative is choosing the life of a social justice warrior, but it's going to be an uphill battle, and I doubt you'll end up happier because of it.

This is a sticky topic, so please let me extend an olive branch. I know what it's like to be on the other side, to be forced to adapt in unfair ways. I lived in Honduras for eight years, and I had to give up many things to fit in with their society. Some of it was small stuff, like not playing cards because, in that culture, they associated cards with reckless debauchery. Americans don't see it that way, but I would be a fool to protest my own beliefs in that scenario. Another form of discrimination I experienced in Honduras was that the white man always pays extra. Taxis cost more, legal paperwork costs more, and government officials demand bribes every chance they get. I experienced unfairness in a plethora of different ways, but getting angry about it would have been a losing strategy.

Think about it. How many self-professed victims live a thriving and fulfilling life? How many legends were created from people feeling sorry for themselves?

It's great that we live in an era of equality. I love that about our generation. But somewhere along the line, we started focusing on the inequalities instead of the abundance of opportunities, which has turned us into victims. We become ineffective, bitter, and angry when we forget how truly blessed we are. You are in control of your results and the outcome of your life. Take responsibility for whatever is holding you back from greatness and deal with it appropriately.

ACTION STEPS

1. LIST TWO AREAS OF ENTITLEMENT YOU NEED TO CRUSH.

....

....

....

2. WHAT'S YOUR PLAN TO CRUSH THEM?

....

....

....

....

....

....

....

....

....

....

> "
>
> Life is 10% what happens to you and 90% how you react to it.
>
> — **CHARLES R. SWINDOLL**

CHAPTER FIVE

MASTER YOUR PRIORITIES AND POTENTIAL

Fact: what you focus on will grow. If you focus on the most impactful activities, you will win. If you value everything equally, you will lose. We are far more capable than we realize, but we have to live a life of intention. Otherwise, we will wander aimlessly and achieve nothing.

Mastering Your Priorities

Mastering your priorities starts with the following question: "What is truly important to me?" Maybe you can relate to this—I often fall into the trap of living out someone else's life. Somewhere in my subconscious, there's a little man telling me what's important and what isn't; but unfortunately, that little man is typically wrong. Prioritizing starts with taking the time to figure out what *your* priorities are in the first place, so you can then relentlessly focus on them. You'll have to crush your time wasters and fear of commitment to make this possible.

In my busiest season in college, I took double the recommended course load, wrote and produced a commercially distributed music album, and still had enough time to serve my church eighteen hours a week. Despite the lengthy to-do list, I was able to sleep a solid nine hours every night. Now, before you assume I've been gifted with a superhuman, high-capacity gene, I can assure you, I have not. I believe anyone can have a similar result if they're willing to live a life of intention.

Growing up, I was embarrassed by how much sleep I needed compared to the people around me. However, since I knew I was wired this way, I prioritized sleep for this season so I could execute everything else at the highest level. I put my needs first so I could get everything else done. I decided nine hours of sleep would help me be a happy and productive person, so I gave it to myself. From there, I figured out how to crush the rest of it in the least amount of time.

This forced my brain to come up with creative solutions. My first realization was that I needed to rethink how I studied. I no longer had much time in the evenings because of the sheer number of classes I was taking, plus other commitments. I figured out if I got a full night's rest, showed up to class fifteen minutes early, read the chapter, vigorously took notes during the lecture, then reviewed them on the way to my next class, I could forgo the studying I once needed. Repetition was the key to this strategy, and it resulted in a GPA of 3.84, despite my lengthy list of responsibilities.

While I was dialed in on crushing my priorities, my next-door neighbor managed half the responsibilities I had, and still struggled to get even *six* hours of sleep a night. The myth is that time is the issue, but more often than not, it's really just about how we *use* our time. Prioritize your most essential tasks, then stick to the plan without deviation. Most people who complain about never having enough time haven't invested the time to figure out where they're wasting it. Until they do, they will never get their time back and will spend their lives exhausted.

Living a life of intention produces powerful results and is one of the keys to finding purpose even in mundane activities. Millions if not billions of people aimlessly wander around the earth exhausted, lost, and mildly annoyed because they don't consistently define what's important to them. It's no wonder they struggle to find meaning in routine. There's nothing to hope for except for trivial dopamine hits found in meaningless pleasures.

In contrast, if you live a life of intention, you just might get what you want.

So what's most important to you? What will your "no matter what" be? Before continuing, I'd like you to ask yourself the following questions:

- What are my needs?
- What do I want more of?
- What do I need less of?

Figure out what you, your body, and your emotional well-being needs, then prioritize it relentlessly. If you physically schedule it in your calendar, you'll be much more likely to follow through with it and achieve it.

In that season, my priority was sleep. Currently, it's devoting a solid hour every morning to reading scriptures and books that build my knowledge and confidence. I love my life when I prioritize things that make me a better person. When I work on myself for the first hour of each morning, the rest of my day goes seamlessly. Whatever it is for you, schedule it, then prioritize it relentlessly.

Would you give up a comfortable job for a high income? Or, would you prefer to give up a big salary to spend more time with your family? Define your needs, then find the steps to obtain them. Crushing your priorities needs to be a consistent theme throughout your life. It's easy to skip this step or put it on the back burner, but I can assure you, from personal experience, that it's worth it. I am happier with the results when I take a couple of hours a month to recenter and refocus on what's important for that specific season. Some seasons, I'll cut out media entirely—no TV, Facebook, or movies for five to six months at a time. That way, I can declutter my mind and focus on more valuable tasks. In other seasons, my wife and I spend a relatively large amount of time watching TV shows, because it's one of the things we enjoy doing together.

The *How* Question

Once you've defined your priorities, it's time to make the necessary steps toward mastering them. This is often easier said than done. Many things will block you from where you need to be. Your friends might hinder you from pursuing the growth you desire, and you might not be clear on what the next right step is. Heck, you might even start to doubt yourself or doubt that the change you want is even possible. I want to provide you with a powerful tool to help you crush your own limiting beliefs. I call this tool the *how* question. I have found that the *how* question is the most efficient way to overcome preconceived notions of what you are or are not capable of. Not only will it boost your confidence, but it will also help you come up with creative solutions faster.

I started using the *how* question six years ago, and it has been a life-changer for me. It was a small change: I substituted the phrase, "Can I do _____?" to "*How* can I do _____?" and this has made all the difference. I stopped asking myself, "Can I?" because the answer would usually stop there: No, I cannot. Instead, I now ask myself, "*How* can I?" because this forces my brain to find a solution. It's a solution-based question instead of a permission-based question. This led me to a monumental discovery: our brains are much more powerful than we realize. It was fascinating how I used to instinctively tell myself "no" when the simplest "*How* can I?" would give me the solution I need.

Pick any problematic obstacle and ask yourself, "*How* can I _____?" The answer will most likely come right to you. Let's look at some "I can't" statements to test this theory:

"I can't spend time with my friends because I'm too busy at work."
"I can't travel the world because it would compromise my other goals."
"I can't be happy under these circumstances."
"I can't win. The cards are stacked against me, and it doesn't matter what I do."

These statements are phrased as if the door to success has been closed for you. But that's not true. You don't have to accept defeat like this.

I'll prove it to you:

"*How* can I prioritize time with my friends and still get my work done?"
"*How* can I travel the world and still hit my goals?"
"*How* can I reframe what just happened and choose happiness?"
"*How* can I be victorious despite this recent defeat?"

Do you see how different that felt? Changing those statements to *how* questions gave us the power to take ground in the midst of adversity.

Most modern medicine is centered on triggering systems in our bodies to fight diseases instead of fighting the disease directly. The same principle applies with our brains. Instead of succumbing to the stress, ask yourself the right questions and let your brain do the heavy lifting on its own. I encourage you to make this pivotal switch in your language, starting today.

Mastering Your Potential

A high-performing friend of mine told me that when he has a seemingly unsolvable challenge, a Kryptonite to overcome, he reviews the challenge just before he goes to bed so his mind will process the issue while he sleeps. He claimed that he has had great results by letting his brain passively process tasks for him. I'll be honest, when I first heard this, I received it with a mild amount of skepticism. But I was far too curious to ignore the suggestion, so I tried it out.

To understand the story I am about to share, I should mention that on the weekends, I am a sound engineer for a church in Dallas. One of my responsibilities is to create a quality broadcast mix for viewers at home. A lot goes into translating live music into a home environment; I have to work with everything from compression to live pitch correction. At the beginning, I was struggling to create a million-dollar sound on a ten-thousand-dollar budget, and I was running into plenty of technical limitations. I sorted out most of the challenges, but I was still having a hard time capturing the energy of the live room for the viewers at home.

To test my friend's theory, I reviewed the problem that night, right before I went to sleep. Then, to ensure my brain wouldn't keep me up all night, I did some simple breathing exercises where I inhaled and exhaled slowly to calm myself. I went to sleep, and woke up with a plug-and-play solution. I couldn't believe it! For the sake of this book, I won't explain the nerdy details, but I solved one of my biggest problems and did it while sleeping, with almost no effort.

This is a great way to work smarter, not harder. It's like cheating on a test but without the fear of getting caught. It's amazing! I have tried this many times, and although I don't always wake up with the perfect solution, I frequently have the next few steps figured out for me.

This reinforces my belief that our brains are far more capable than we realize. We think we know our limitations, but the truth is that we have so many tools in our toolbelt which remain unused that can help us to master our potential. That's why it's so important to surround yourself with capable people who want the best for you. We need people who are several steps ahead of us in life as proof that there is more to be had, that it is possible to optimize your life in ways that will get you better results. Babies do not know they can talk until they hear us speaking, and have no idea they can walk until they see us walking. Once a child knows it's possible, learning to walk and talk becomes their obsession. They're willing to push past the bruises of failure because they know it's possible.

Sonar technology was developed through studying dolphins, and flight came from watching birds. We have made substantial progress in science and technology by studying nature and then replicating it. That's one of the reasons why I believe it's so hard for people in the inner cities to break out of the poverty cycle. They are replicating what they see around them. If you're surrounded by limited thinking and negative behaviors, you'll most likely adapt to that way of life. If you don't have solid role models, you will grow out of your "childish" dreams of reaching for the stars. Without examples to follow, it's extremely difficult to believe anything more is possible. I have had many moments where I am tempted to give up on my dreams, but seeing my friends push past their own belief barriers gave me the courage to press on.

Limited thinking limits us. If the people around us believe that something is impossible, we will most likely believe the same. And when someone dares to question that notion, someone will inevitably shut them down. Don't let someone telling you your dream isn't *realistic* dictate your reality. If you surround yourself with people who can fly, you will eventually join them in the skies. The question now becomes, *how* can you surround yourself with competent people who want the best for you? *How* can you prioritize growth in your life?

Here's a business-world example. I love business, because it's blatantly obvious who is implementing winning strategies and who is giving in to their limiting beliefs. In most areas of life, it's tough to gauge how well you're doing. For example, it's hard to quantify your parenting skills with measurable data. Likewise, there isn't a chart or spreadsheet that can track your progress in becoming a better human. Business, however, makes personal growth quantifiable because your development can be tracked by profitability. In the words of Warren Buffett, "The more you learn, the more you earn." People can brag all they want to about how successful they are, but the proof is in how profitable their business is. In sales, I know exactly how good I am by the results I produce. The more books I read, the better I perform.

The Self-Sufficiency Trap

Mastering your priorities and potential can keep you from falling into what I call the self-sufficiency trap—inefficiency caused by doing everything yourself.

From an early age, I was taught to do everything by myself. I was taught to cook, clean, and take care of myself. I even learned how to change the brakes in my car, all to be self-reliant and save a few hundred bucks. This type of resourcefulness is helpful when at the bottom of the totem pole, but it has diminishing returns when advancing the social and economic ladder. Society has reinforced this shortcoming by praising me for being scrappy, but it's all a lie. The most successful people on the planet are *not* self-sufficient. Billionaires don't operate like that. They focus on the things that matter most and rely on thousands of other people to manage the details. They don't need to know the inner workings of every facet of their companies because self-reliance is serial inefficiency.

There was a time in my life when I would celebrate my friends for their self-reliance. "Man! You saved three thousand dollars by learning how to fix your plumbing and electrical issues. That's great!" Please don't get me wrong—I love overachievers who are constantly learning new things, but there comes a point where utilizing another's time or skills will help you win faster.

If our focus is on the cost of a task, it's easy to justify most of these habits. But if we account for the indirect costs of the time it took to learn this skill and perform the task, as well as the mental bandwidth we sacrificed, it becomes apparent just how wasteful this mental framework can be. This is especially true when we do all this work for a skill we may only use once or twice a year.

Cultivating your genius and then enlisting the help of others is more effective the farther you get in life, and The Mayo Clinic is an excellent example of this.

The Mayo brothers pioneered the way for physicians to specialize in healthcare. Initially, Dr. Will and Dr. Charlie left general medicine to specialize in surgery together. They specialized even further when they realized that was still too broad of a subject, each taking half of the body to focus on. Eventually, they hired a massive staff of physicians, each with a narrow focus, collectively mastering individual segments of the disease spectrum. They made giant strides in their respective fields and advanced the world's knowledge of the body because they got more repetition of the same types of cases than other doctors at the time. Seeing the same kinds of sicknesses every day made their learning curve much shorter, which led to many medical breakthroughs. Even two hundred years later, their hospital is still one of the leading communities of research and development.[2]

While writing this book, I have been reintroduced to a strategy of prioritization that I think will help you steer clear of this trap. In their book, *Who Not How*, co-founder and CEO of Strategic Coach, Dan Sullivan, and Dr. Benjamin Hardy explain their formula for achieving big goals and accelerated growth through teamwork.[3]

There are three applications to consider when implementing *Who Not How*: Skillset, Capacity, and Value of Time.

Skillset:

I have a friend who took a shortcut in life by shooting straight to the top and conniving his way into the company of the world's elite. Instead of figuring out *how* to become successful, he used the *Who Not How* concept and found his *who*. In other words, he found people who were already successful and could teach him. As a broke teenager, the only way he could get to the information he needed was to volunteer at conferences. He couldn't afford a Tony Robbins or a John Maxwell conference, so he volunteered as a stagehand at many different events. This enabled him to inundate himself with the wisdom that helped him build an INC 5000 company in his early twenties. Very few people achieve *anything* so noteworthy by this age, but he saved himself a lot of time by finding his *who*.

---

[2] Markel, D. H. (2018, June 29). *The brilliant brothers behind the Mayo Clinic*. PBS. Retrieved January 15, 2022, from https://www.pbs.org/newshour/health/the-brilliant-brothers-behind-the-mayo-clinic

[3] Sullivan, D. (2020). *Who not how*. Hay House.

I love stories like this, because they illustrate how we can get almost anything we want if we are willing to put ourselves out there and go for it. On the flip side, I can't help but wonder how many paid waiters and waitresses have had similar exposure to the same people but didn't value the information enough to listen and implement it. Someone somewhere knows the secret to every single problem. Find that person, and figure out how to convince them to help you develop your skillset.

Capacity:

If you try to learn everything, you won't be very good at anything, and if you try to figure things out by yourself, it will take forever. This is why it's important to determine your capacity for tasks. Marketing expert Gary Vaynerchuk once said, "There's no sixteen-step formula to becoming Beyonce." We all have three to five things that we're naturally good at. Focus on these things.

The trap is that we give so much attention to improving fifty of our weaknesses that we neglect to perfect our strengths. Focus on developing your strengths, then hire someone with different strengths to solve your problems. Smart, driven people tend to recognize each other, so finding your *whos* is easiest when you're on your A-game. The people who are where you want to be need friends and competent employees, both of which are hard to come by. Be that competent person, and chances are that the very people you need are looking for a person like you.

For example, I have no business being a mechanic. Could I figure out how to fix my own car? Yes. Would it make me feel like a badass? Yes, it would. I selfishly want to prove that I'm a high-capacity person, but the cost is too high. It would take too long, taking time away from my other priorities. Though I have no doubt I could learn any number of random skills, the question I ask myself is: will this serve me in the long run? When it comes to fixing cars, the answer is: absolutely not. I may deceive myself into thinking it would help me in the short term, but I know my willpower and cognitive capabilities are finite, so I would rather invest them in mastering my strengths. Instead of wasting my brainpower on unnecessary things, I focus on the three to five things I can become exceptional at. Find the three to five things you're good at, focus on them, and you will build positive momentum that will lead you from victory to victory.

Value of Time:

Valuing my time has been a recent area of growth for me, and it may be something you struggle with as well. I had previously conditioned myself to be self-reliant, but I've found it's a losing battle. I am finite. I have a limited amount of time on Earth, so I am choosing to spend it well.

If getting ahead in your life is important to you, I suggest you outsource any task that costs you less than your hourly rate so you can focus on perfecting your craft. If you make $50 an hour, don't clean your home or mow your lawn, because those are simple tasks that can be offloaded for $10-20 an hour. If it's something you enjoy doing, then fine, do it. But if the only reason you're doing those tasks is that you've always felt like you had to, you're not valuing your time well.

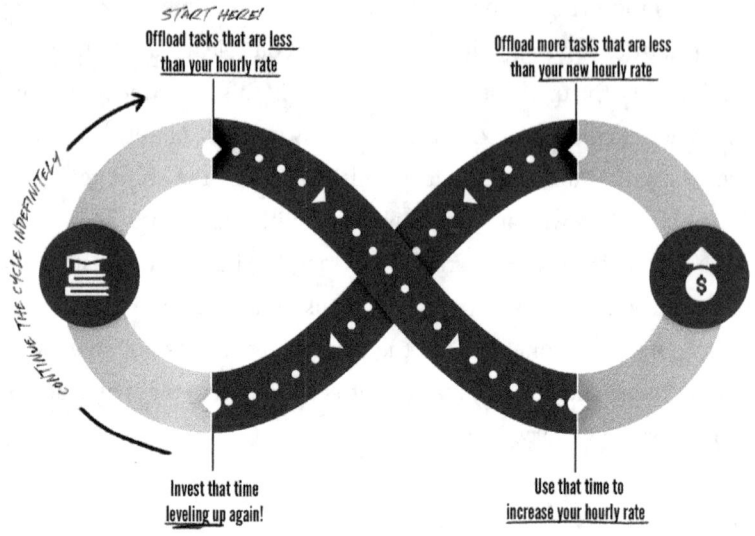

Let's take this a little further. Let's say you could figure out how to make $60 an hour and could save twelve hours a week by outsourcing cooking, cleaning, and lawn care. That would essentially give you an extra $2,880 per month of your time back. Having ready-made food delivered and outsourcing the rest of your mundane chores might only cost you an additional $900 a month, so you would save $1,980 a month by taking these tasks off of your to-do list.

I hired a cook to shop and cook 28 meals for my wife and me every week, and it only costs me one hundred dollars plus the cost of the groceries. The four hundred dollars a month I invest for my meals to be taken care of gets me well over two thousand dollars worth of my time back. Now I'm sure you're wondering how I could hire someone to grocery shop and cook all of my meals for so little money. The reason is that the cook is extremely efficient and has developed a remarkable talent for it. If I were to cook that many meals, it would take me all day, and I would dirty every dish in my house twice. But because she's been perfecting her craft for longer than I've been alive, she can handle it in a few short hours.

This is an exponential game, not a linear one. If offloading tasks and creating passive income can help you increase your time by 40 percent, you can probably cut the time it takes to get to the next income bracket in half. That extra 40 percent might have tripled your overall disposable time, with which you can invest in figuring out how to get to the next level. The same applies to increasing your income. A 40 percent increase in revenue might double your disposable funds, which will give you significantly more time back, which you can invest back into generating more income faster. Leveling up is a game played in the margins, so do everything you can to increase those margins for every area of your life.

Now, these calculations were made with the assumption that you are in a production-based job where producing more pays you more. If your job isn't like that, I recommend finding one fast. Very few ultra-successful people got there on a fixed salary, and even those who do eventually become wealthy that way typically take their whole lives to get there. Control your time, and you will eventually control your income.

There are limitless opportunities to leverage your time besides the three basic categories I mentioned above. I've found one way to leverage my time value of money is to leverage the currency deferential when outsourcing tasks. That's the allure behind companies like Fiverr and Upwork. I can get a graphic designer from Pakistan or Turkey to create promotional material and cover designs for around $40, when it might cost ten times that amount to produce locally here in the US. They're willing to do this because their cost of living is 18-20 percent of ours. It's a win-win situation. I'm happy because I got a deal, and they're happy because they're charging me more than they could locally. The money goes a lot farther for both parties. It's a win-win situation.

I'm bringing this up because I believe it's important to squash self-reliance and self-sufficiency. It's an easy trap to fall for because of how impressive it sounds, but it's limiting our effectiveness. Let's say you were to meet an older gentleman who has been self-sufficient most of his life. He might have a lot of things going for him—a wife, a family, and a respectable living. He's probably proud that he can fix his car, fix his house, and take care of his surroundings well, and that's admirable. But here's the issue. The man I just described lives on an average street, has a typical job and lives a typical life. There's nothing wrong with living a typical life—in fact, most people do, which is why it's called *typical*. But what's the point of knowing how to do a million things if it doesn't lead you to an *extraordinary* life? If you're trying to be good at everything, you will spread yourself so thin that you won't be truly *great* at anything.

Contrast that with people like Bill Gates. When he built Microsoft, Bill Gates excelled at one thing. He was great at leading techies to create good products. He never started a T-shirt line, because that would be a colossal waste of his brainpower. He became so good at that one thing that he could charge thousands of dollars an hour for it, and eventually, he made billions from it. He could charge so much for his time because he solved problems for millions of people.

In other words, he was very good at adding value to people's lives. He prioritized his genius and then surrounded himself with capable people to handle the rest. And the fascinating part about this is that he wasn't very good at coding or building computers himself. In fact, his first product was created by someone he didn't even know. Yet, he built one of the most successful technology companies by attracting and leading the right people.

If the most successful people specialize, why should we be different? We may not be the next Bill Gates, but we can definitely increase our impact by consistently recouping our time and investing it back into developing our primary skillsets. Why not focus on solving a couple of problems so effectively that you can afford to trade for someone else's time to solve the rest of your needs? As much as my ego would love nothing more than to be self-sufficient, unless there is a zombie apocalypse and I am the only one left, I will be better served by focusing on my strengths.

Frankly, I'm reminded of this every time I play foosball or Mario Kart, because I'm hilariously bad at both. I don't try to learn everything anymore, because I'm self-aware enough to know where to focus my efforts.

Do you see how developing your strengths is a far better strategy than cutting coupons or becoming a jack-of-all-trades? Don't worry about everything. Focus on the few things you're good at, and you won't have to worry about the rest. Treat your time like your most valuable asset, and it will be worth a fortune. This will lead you to even bigger opportunities.

If you're struggling to implement the *Who Not How* concept, I encourage you to start asking yourself powerful questions like:

- *How* can I get 5 hours of my time back?
- *How* can I invest my time instead of spending it?
- *How* can I shorten my learning curve?

Ask yourself the right questions, and you'll find the right solutions. I mentioned how I am doing it as a sales rep, but I know people who do it through acquiring assets that pay them every month, i.e., cash flow. They do the work once and get paid for decades. Now that cash (passive income) is flowing in regardless of their activities, they are free to make bolder moves with their career. And by leveling up there, they now have more time or a higher hourly rate, so that they can continue the cycle. It's a self-feeding machine.

Prioritization in Action

Life hacks are everywhere when you look for them. For example, my wife and I have been talking about the possibility of moving to Mexico, where our money will go further. Their cost of living is roughly a third of ours, so not only would that potentially free up some of my time, but we could live on the beach like kings for far less than it costs to live in Dallas, Texas. Since I work remotely on the phone, I would still get paid in American dollars and could triple my buying power. You might consider something like this, or you could even try applying for a remote job based in the UK since, as of the time of publication of this book, Pounds Sterling is much stronger than USD. The opportunities are endless when you're willing to create them. Yes, it will involve sacrifice, but it's often worth it.

If working less is your priority, figure out how to accomplish that. I have some friends who wanted to homeschool their children so they would have a better education than they did. To get their time back, they purchased a duplex. The rent they charge on the other half of the duplex pays for them to live on their half for free. By offloading one of their largest expenses, the husband (who is a contractor) doesn't have to work as much and can help his wife teach their children. I think this is a really sweet way to invest in their children instead of being wage-slaves.

My wife and I have made similar choices. One of our priorities is to acquire cash-flow-producing assets before we have kids, so we aren't trapping ourselves in a tight financial situation. I don't want us to be stressed about bills once we have little rugrats running around. We want the ability to spend ample amounts of time with our kids. I also don't want my life to be just about me. Poor planning will put me in a position where I'm forced to spend all my time caring for my needs, which would be inadvertently selfish. For now, I am focused on getting ahead so I can invest my time and resources helping others.

Mastering your priorities is about defining your non-negotiables and asking the *how* question. This helps you develop creative solutions instead of settling for what everyone else is doing, because let's face it—what everyone else is doing isn't working very well. What you focus on will improve, so focus on what you really want and let all the other stuff take a back seat. Most people don't make an effort to prioritize what they value, so life takes them by storm and they live an unhappy existence. But it doesn't have to be like that. You can make better choices that will produce better results.

Time is not the issue. Circumstances are also not the issue. Failing to plan is the issue. Once you commit to mastering your life, everything else will take its rightful place. Mastering your priorities and potential is all about killing your time wasters and committing to the things that will make you a better human. Focus on that, and success will follow.

Are you still feeling a little stuck? It could be because you still need to crush procrastination. The next chapter will show you how.

ACTION STEPS

LIST YOUR TWO BIGGEST CONCERNS AND TAKE TEN MINUTES TO ASK YOURSELF, "HOW CAN I .... ?"

How can I _____

How can I _____

CHAPTER SIX

CRUSH YOUR PROCRASTINATION

As sales reps, my friends and I know all too well the true cost of procrastination. We see it every day, all the time, and it shows no signs of stopping. Procrastination at its very core fascinates me. When other people procrastinate, we acknowledge it's a problem. But when *we* procrastinate, it's a different story. We craft compelling explanations for our own indecisiveness. We are so persuasive with ourselves that procrastination becomes the only logical and wise choice.

For my job, most of the people I talk to come to me for help building their businesses and achieving their dreams. It's truly an honor to have these meaningful conversations every day. One of the first questions I ask them is, "How long have you wanted to do this?" Typically they'll tell me it's been anywhere from five to ten years, but occasionally I'll meet someone who has been dreaming about their particular goal for longer than I've been alive. I love strategizing with people about their dreams, but my struggle is that for many, no matter how well our planning session goes, they will end the conversation with something to the effect of, "Nate, this is amazing, but obviously, I need to sleep on it first." Procrastination is their default response. I would support them talking things slowly, if it weren't for the fact that they have been doing that for years or even decades without any substantial progress. I often have conversations with people I last spoke with years ago who still haven't taken their first step. It's all talk and no action. I've found that if I try to help them a second time, they will get excited with me again—and then still procrastinate on their dreams. It's tough to watch.

Indecision, procrastination, and dillydallying are truly harmful. We know that intellectually, but that doesn't keep us from pushing decisions and tasks off for another time—and when we do that, we never really get the job done. "Maybe" is not a decision. "Maybe" never happens; it's passive, and will cost you dearly. "No" decisions are much better than "maybes" because a "no" forces you to shut that door permanently and move on to the next decision. If you have a dream but make a firm decision not to pursue that dream at this time, it frees you up to create other opportunities elsewhere.

If you indulge yourself by leaving the door to every opportunity slightly ajar, you are deceiving yourself with the illusion that you will have the time and mental fortitude to revisit all of these decisions "one day." You're lying to yourself, and you're placing yourself in decision-making limbo.

As a college student selling books door-to-door, I noticed the stark difference between how financially successful people make decisions and how everybody else makes decisions. When I was with successful people, in their million-dollar homes with their indoor pools and all their fancy luxuries, I loved that they didn't give excuses or fancy explanations. They always told me either "yes" or "no."

This is very different from the way most people operate. We frequently say things like, "I need to think about it," or, "Let me talk to my husband." Whatever the particular phrasing is, we often can't get ourselves to say "no" if we are unsure. Trust me—a good decision in the moment is better than a perfect decision once it's too late.

If you procrastinate on thousands of decisions, how do you expect to go back and revisit all of them? It's impossible. There is no earthly way to make that work. That's why ultra-successful people are better at saying "yes" or "no." Indecision will cost you a fortune in time, money, and impact. The people with the most results are the ones who take the most action. It's as simple as that.

I have had many friends ask me for stock market advice throughout the years. With great curiosity, they tell me, "Nate, I want to learn about investing. I want to make things happen in my life!" Their words seem to indicate they're ready to take action, but I've found that no amount of education or support will get most of them to do any of it. Education is fun, but things change when they have to put their money where their mouth is.

On several occasions, I have invested time holding their hands through every step, from detailed explanations to downloading trading apps to showing them my trading accounts. Every time, they've balked at the last minute. I even tried guaranteeing their money in the unlikely event they lost any, but to no avail.

One said, "Of course, I will 100 percent do that! I just need to talk to my wife first." Others said they needed to "take a look at their budget" first. As far as I know, all of them are finally in the market today, but most of them took three to five years before making the plunge. Their indecision cost them more in opportunity loss than they will ever know.

Procrastination limits your effectiveness and slows you down. You can't reason it away and you can't educate it away. So how do you deal with it? What do you do? I've spent the last ten years thinking about this, and I've arrived at some core truths on the subject. First of all: you cannot fix this problem by talking about it. Action is the only solution, so you must force yourself to make decisions quicker if you want to develop that muscle. Procrastination is essentially saying "I don't trust myself." If you don't trust yourself, the only way forward is to make as many little decisions and as many little mistakes as possible so you grow to trust yourself with more significant decisions later on.

Let's say you're at the grocery store and you're struggling to decide which ice cream to buy. Instead of blocking the aisle and fogging the glass up, make a decision—any decision. Then, let's say later on that day there's a task you're about to add to your to-do list—why not just do it right then? Knock it out. Do it now, take action, and you will start to trust yourself more.

Overcoming procrastination is important for every facet of our lives. Growing up, my older brother and I were very competitive. I was fifteen, he was eighteen, and we both wanted to bulk up. You know, the typical macho thing. We both went to the gym, but quickly, my older brother started saying things like, "I just don't feel like I know what I'm doing yet. I want to do my research and figure out the best ways to build muscle before I keep lifting. It's the safe thing to do." I think you know how this ends. Even though I wasn't a fitness guru, action and continuous improvement got me much further than "research" ever would have. Five years later, I was the powerlifting champion, and my brother was just as scrawny as the day we started. So please, don't convince yourself that the best thing to do is nothing. Although patience is a virtue, procrastination is definitely not.

Not only does procrastination prolong decision-making, but it also slows your learning curve down. Here is a poker analogy, in the hopes of better explaining this concept: two of my friends were professional poker players, and they both developed their skills by playing multiple online cash games—simultaneously. They told me it used to drive them nuts whenever they would be in Las Vegas casinos and see outstanding poker players make childish blunders based on emotions or boredom. They believe talented players make simple mistakes because they are playing an extremely slow game. Each move took minutes instead of the split-second decisions they were used to in the online arena. The benefit of playing simultaneous games is that you will make your mistakes quickly and avoid developing poor habits. If you constantly play and constantly fail, you will quickly learn from your mistakes—or go broke trying. This forces you to make better choices and protects you from childish blunders.

Procrastination is a silent killer. Much like carbon monoxide, it's barely detectable, and all it needs is a little time to destroy you from the inside out. Taking the easy way out here and allowing a little indecision over there creates a habit that—compounded daily for years on end—will paralyze you.

Procrastination is just as expensive as a smoking addiction. If you are a pack-a-day smoker, $6.25 doesn't sound like it would impact your future. Wrong! Think Again. That one habit costs $2,292 a year.[4] If you invested that at 7 percent interest for 20 years, you would have around $100,000. That's just if you quit one crummy little habit. If you took the same example and invested that at a 20 percent compound interest over the same time frame, you would have roughly $513,474. And if you think 20 percent returns on your money is "unrealistic" and exaggerated, I kindly suggest you start implementing these healthy habits so you can find someone to teach you how to make your money work for you.

The adverse effects of smoking don't stop there. I've read numerous surveys that indicated smokers who smoke a pack a day spend anywhere from one to two hours a day smoking. That's roughly 365-730 hours a year smoking. In a 20 year period, that's between 7,300 and 14,600 hours you can't get back.

If you devoted the five hundred grand and the roughly 10,950 additional hours to improving your craft and investing in yourself, the reward would be in the millions. That's the true cost of that "little" bad habit.

Procrastination works the same way. It isn't just limiting your effectiveness; it's also affecting your physical health. Imagine how much

---

[4] McCann, A. (2022, January 12). *The real cost of smoking by state.* WalletHub. Retrieved January 16, 2022, from https://wallethub.com/edu/the-financial-cost-of-smoking-by-state/9520

healthier you'd be if you never procrastinated on your workouts and always ate right? Imagine how much less stressed you'd be if you never put yourself in a situation where you had to scramble last minute? How much more leisure time would you have if you made decisions concisely instead of avoiding them?

Most people agree that smoking is a bad habit, but unfortunately, we don't see procrastination in the same light, and it's costing us dearly. We're often not even aware of it, allowing it to roam freely and devour us as it pleases. Even though it's undoubtedly costing us more, we wouldn't fight procrastination like we would fight a thief breaking into our home. It's so much easier to fight for something that's being taken away from us than it is to fight for something we never had. Missed opportunities don't sting as much as loss does.

Children are a great example of this. If you give a small child three cookies and then take one back, the child will kick and scream because they feel the loss of that third cookie. But if they never knew that cookie existed, they would have gone about their day with two cookies, none the wiser.

We are the same way. We typically don't fight procrastination because its effects are intangible. Let's change that. Here are four ways we procrastinate, and four ways to wage war on this Kryptonite.

Endless Possibilities

The first way we procrastinate is by giving ourselves endless amounts of time with endless possibilities. With this as our baseline, progress is arduous. I fell into this trap when I first started investing in real estate.

My thought process went something like this: "Well, let's see here. I could do single-family homes, duplexes, quadplexes, or apartment buildings. Quadplexes seem like a great place to start because there's less risk if I can't fill a unit, so let's start with that. Or...I could skip the housing market and go straight to office complexes or self-storage, because there's even less risk of client turnover. Well...do I want to focus on properties that build my monthly cash flow, or would it be better to do deals that would grow equity faster and then flip those properties into larger buildings that would give us more cash flow later on?"

Analysis paralysis was crushing me. Each of these opportunities would be incredible, but I wasted over a year on pointless behavior because I over-explored my options. I've heard it said that you should measure twice and cut once. I agree, but most of us measure a hundred times to cut once. It's unnecessary. It's in a self-protective effort to avoid painful mistakes, yes, but it's also taking that concept too far. Remember that making a good decision in the moment is better than waiting for the perfect decision. Fear tells us that spending more time on research will save us pain, but it costs far more than a mistake would have.

Just do it! Do it scared, do it now, do it without all the information you think you need. Do it in spite of what people think or say. By crushing your procrastination, your learning curve will improve significantly.

Perfectionism

The second reason we procrastinate is due to perfectionism. We all want to do things well but fall into the trap of wasting endless hours on details that breed insignificant results.

One of my sisters is really good at prioritizing tasks that produce results and ignoring the rest. By twenty-one, she had successfully rehabbed thirteen rental properties that she now manages. I decided to tag along for one of her rehab projects. She kept asking me to do simple tasks—scrape the peeling paint off a windowpane, powerwash the siding, etc. She consistently asked for the bare minimum, but my perfectionism would kick into gear and I would waste hours completing the task because I wanted it to look immaculate.

She would then come back and tell me, "Nate, you don't have to be that thorough. Just scrape whatever comes off easily, and be done with it."

Not making things perfect kills my inner perfectionist. I want everything to be amazing, but the one aspect I was ignoring in that scenario was speed. No matter how mediocre or spectacular my paint job looked by the end of it, that rental would rent for the same standard amount. If we spent twice the time making things perfect, we would end up with half the rental units on the market. If I continued to give in to perfectionism, my efforts would be wasted.

Putting time constraints and dates on projects helps me crush perfectionism and push things out the door. This book is an excellent example. It's the first book I've written, and I could have spent an endless amount of time writing it. English and grammar aren't strengths of mine, so if I didn't put a deadline on it, I could have spent the next decade going through my manuscript again and again, fact-checking, correcting, and going down the perfectionist rabbit hole. Would it make my book better? Potentially. But then I would run the risk of having the best book that no one gets a chance to read. Putting a time constraint forces me to finish what I can and to get help with the things I can't do. By hiring an editor—someone who edits for a living—I can lean on their expertise and escape the hamster wheel of endless rewrites.

There are two paradigms you could follow. The first is perfection. If you're living in the paradigm of perfection, you are motivated by external sources screaming at you to be "perfect." This is a horrible place to live. You never know what "perfect" looks like, so you will continue to exhaust yourself, reaching for an unreachable and hypothetical benchmark. It's exhausting, because there is no end in sight. There is no rest for a perfectionist. You will live here forever.

Contrast that with the second paradigm: excellence. Excellence is characterized by consistently doing your best while giving yourself grace when you mess up. Excellence provides a similar result, but without the self-inflicted pain. You can look back at your achievements and smile. Excellence is joyful. Perfectionism is a slave driver.

The funny thing about perfectionism is that it can bring about beautiful results. Perfectionism can get you to the very top. It can motivate you to work harder than everyone else and achieve more and more and more. These results can be so enticing that it's easy to ignore the poison on the back end. The dark side to perfectionism is that it keeps you longer than it should and never lets you enjoy what you achieved, thus driving you into the ground. Perfectionism is a short-term strategy. It might help you for a few years, but you will inevitably fall short of someone who has a much healthier view of work.

Decision Fatigue

The third reason we procrastinate is due to decision fatigue. If you need to make hundreds of decisions in a single day, you might not make the sharpest decisions toward the end of it all.

An easy way to alleviate decision fatigue is to minimize the number of decisions you're opening yourself up to on any given day. For example, if you had to make a new decision every morning on whether or not to brush your teeth, get dressed, or drive to work, you would be exhausted by the end of each day. By deciding all of these mundane activities once and for all, you are freeing up mental bandwidth for new decisions.

I have a friend who is a champion when it comes to moderation. He concluded that it's much easier to cut something out of his life entirely than it is to moderate it constantly. For instance, when regulating his sugar intake, he realized it would take less energy to completely cut out soda, sweets, and desserts than it would be to cut them back a little, tracking his intake all the time. By drawing a hard line with sugar, he wasn't wasting time asking himself whether he should eat the cupcake or not. He knew the answer was *no*, so he avoided torturing himself with the decision. Our brains are good with creative loopholes if it involves poor behaviors. Sometimes the best thing you can do is to make an all-encompassing decision once, so you avoid making the same decision daily.

Lack of Knowledge

The fourth reason we procrastinate is due to a lack of knowledge. It's hard to take action when you don't know what to do next.

No matter how impossible the task might seem, there are people out there who have overcome the same Kryptonite that has you under its thumb. There are simple solutions to the problems that have crushed you. However, finding the solution is difficult when everyone around you is struggling with the same problem. There are friend groups, for instance, in which every guy is physically wimpy. Is getting fit really that hard? No, but if your friends don't prioritize healthy behaviors, it's an easy pass for you, too. As the old adage goes, birds of a feather flock together.

If you want to break out of a negative pattern in your life, find someone who's victorious in that area and learn from them. If you're the type of person who says "I'm too busy" or "I could never do that," go surround yourself with people who believe they can do anything. If you're the type of person who takes "no" for an answer and struggles to get to that next level in business, go hang out with consistent winners. Whatever negative belief barrier you have, stop trying to handle it yourself and find someone to guide you.

Bodybuilders think lifting two hundred pounds is easy. Millionaires think making a hundred grand is easy. Even though it's way above my comprehension, molecular biologists probably think whatever the heck it is that *they're* doing is easy, too. My point is that finding a winning solution to the problem life is putting in your way will take forever if you do it all yourself. Once you start treating life as a team sport, it will be much easier to find someone to help you. Someone out there has a system or routine that has helped them get where they are. It's time that you find out what that is.

Living a great life is a lot like building a great company. The best companies in the world have a clear vision and the best people to support them. If that's how businesses flourish, why do we think we can make it on our own? It took a brilliant team to create the iPhone and another great team to support its users when it broke down. We are much more sophisticated than an iPhone, so it stands to reason that we need even more support. Our emotional, spiritual, and physical components work together to help us function, and we need others to build us up and fix us along the way.

The challenge is that it's easier to blame our circumstances instead of acknowledging that our broken systems need repair. In our brokenness, we will quickly surround ourselves with similar-minded people whose belief paradigm is that the system is out to get them. Armed with our new brothers and sisters, we shake our fists at "the system" without addressing the real problem.

But there's hope. Someone with the same circumstances you have has made different decisions and is farther ahead because of it. They didn't blame or complain, but they let go of the things they couldn't control to focus on the things they could. If you surround yourself with those people, instead of viewing yourself as a product of your circumstances, you'll begin to see yourself as a product of your choices—and *everyone* has control over their choices. Controlling the systems of your life is a good thing. Controlling what you can control will get you the positive results you need to move forward, while simultaneously helping you let go of people or situations you can't control.

Suppose you're struggling to make ends meet. This is controllable. You have control of your income. You might not have control of your boss or your job, but you do have control of your income. Be the most dedicated worker at your company, even if you're in an unfair situation. Why? Because you'll be setting yourself apart from the sheep, and eventually, you'll be able to surround yourself with the right people because of it. From there, quit your job if you need to, quit your industry, quit your city. Be the person most willing to pay the price to become an asset to someone who can change your circumstances.

My life is a great example. I love my current work situation, and I got here by following the path of most resistance. I had several work situations where I *was* taken advantage of, lied to, and cheated. But am I caught up in that anymore? Heck no! I got out of there because while I was there, I proved to everyone I was an asset. When the people around me leveled up in life, they eventually brought me with them because they already knew they could count on me. Yes, I ate dirt for a while, but getting through it surrounded me with champions who treat me incredibly well and build me up constantly.

I proactively fill my life with positive people who are actively building themselves. People who know things I want to know. This is the best form of education. For example, when it comes to my job, I currently struggle to help those who haven't held themselves to a high standard of accountability before. I yield to their excuses far too easily and avoid the awkward conversation, when what I should be doing is pressing in because I care about them. I struggle with calling them out in a non-confrontational way without letting them give in to the weaknesses that have held them back.

To overcome my inability to help these people, I will find someone who has more empathy and skill at helping these specific types of people overcome their fear of failure. Instead of allowing myself to stay stuck, I will find others who are farther along in that area than I am, and I will poach their wisdom. It will get me where I need to go faster and enable me to help more people.

Find those with the wisdom you lack to help you crush any Kryptonite you face. Read on to discover how to surround yourself with the right people.

ACTION STEPS

WHAT WAS THE LAST IMPORTANT DECISION YOU PROCRASTINATED?

KNOWING WHAT YOU KNOW NOW, HOW WILL YOU HANDLE THAT KIND OF DECISION IN THE FUTURE?

> "A good decision in the moment is better than a perfect decision once it's too late.
>
> **– NATE HAMBRICK**

CHAPTER SEVEN

MASTER YOUR FRIENDSHIPS

Life is incredibly complicated; there's absolutely no way to figure it all out by yourself, so make sure you have good people in your life to guide you. God created us to live and grow in community with each other, but it's easy to keep people at a distance so we won't get hurt. That becomes a real problem over time. When single individuals live in isolation, they typically end up weird or bitter because they don't have a healthy amount of human interaction and refinement. The longer they live in their weirdness, the stranger they get.

We're all that way. When we isolate, we allow ourselves to drift toward whatever the heck we want at the moment, and it's not healthy. Isolation leads to scenarios like a lady with eighty-seven cats or a guy who eats directly out of the soup can because the dishes have been in the sink for three months.

No one is there to say, "Hey lady, don't you think three cats might be enough?" No one is there to encourage the bachelor that basic hygiene might be a better route. It's so important to have people in our lives to tell us "no" and to push back on our crazy desires. We can relate to fictional characters like Ebenezer Scrooge in *A Christmas Carol* because he internalized pain, isolated himself, and became destructive to himself and others. That wouldn't have happened if he had had friends to guide and refine him.

When I sold life insurance, I frequently visited isolated individuals. Sometimes their residence would have so much trash and cat poop there wasn't a place to set my bag down. I have met hundreds of these people living in complete isolation in one of the most populated cities in the world.

One such gentleman shared his story with me in great detail. He was a veteran, discharged from the service decades ago. There was nothing physically wrong with him, but he went into isolation when he left the service, ballooned up to five hundred pounds, and got on permanent disability due to his weight. The government has been funding this destructive cycle for decades. With his blinds shut, he sits in his tiny apartment, knee-deep in trash, watching television and eating himself to death. He can barely walk because of how much weight he's put on. He's in such bad shape it took him almost ten minutes just to open the door. At first, it seemed like there was nothing physically wrong with him, but he's created an endless list of health conditions due to his poor eating habits and lack of sun and exercise. His medication list was four or five pages long.

Unfortunately, he's not the only person struggling due to lack of community. I've met hundreds of people like this, and I'm sure there are millions more.

That is an extreme example, but we all reject healthy friendships in more minor ways. How often have we left a friend group because of something stupid someone said? How many life decisions have been influenced by our desire to limit interactions with annoying people? If you laughed at that notion, answer me this: have you ever paid extra to shop at Target so you didn't have to interact with the Wal-Mart crowd? Have you ever waited for the delivery man to get back in his car before opening the door, just so you didn't have to say hello? And yes, I mean that humorously. It's funny because it's true. Yes, letting lots of people in your life is messy, but it's also vital to our well-being.

In college, I lived with eight other guys in a small duplex. It was extremely messy, both from a relational perspective and because a few of them were, frankly, nasty. I value maintaining a clean space, so this was beyond frustrating. But amid my frustration, I grew to accept people with poor habits and love people who sometimes made my life uncomfortable. Even though I failed, year after year, to improve these gentlemen's hygiene, I matured in many ways I wouldn't have had I chosen the easy way out and lived alone. My dad calls this "marriage training." It's a willingness to put ourselves in a position to grow. It's hard, it's uncomfortable, but it's also vital to our long-term well-being. And it's beneficial both ways, as I know they also grew from having me in their lives. We need each other's strengths to build us up and show us a better way. We need each other's weaknesses to help us bridge the gap with grace and kindness. We need each other's mistakes so we can learn from them ourselves.

I have more kindness, empathy, and understanding of others because I have chosen to embrace the messiness of those relationships over my temporary comfort. I want to encourage you to do the same.

In the Bible, the apostle Paul talks about being all things to all people. I want to open up a dialogue surrounding this principle. Human beings are fragile, and should be treated with the utmost care. Sometimes that means I must adapt in ways I wish I didn't have to. In a perfect world, I would like to think people would want to cheer me on as I pressed through adversity and built the life of my dreams, but unfortunately, that hasn't been my experience. As a result, I find myself keeping most of my successes to myself. Movies, billboards, and advertisements sell us the lie that if we're successful, everyone will love us. The truth is, the most successful of society are often the most hated, while their unsuccessful counterparts get to live in the anonymity of being average.

The greatest basketball player of all time, Michael Jordan, retired early because of how horribly the media portrayed him. At first, they praised him like a "god" for his super-human talent, but then villainized him for being too tough on his teammates. Magazines tarnished his reputation on their front pages for long enough that he stopped talking with the press at all. This eventually led to his retirement after fifteen seasons, even though many players, like LeBron James and Dirk Nowitzki, played eighteen and twenty-one seasons, respectively. How do people expect the greatest player of all time to behave? Of course, he's aggressive. He's literally the greatest basketball player of all time! Why we believe anyone could be that skilled without a superhuman amount of drive is beyond me.

The way humans think is funny. When a Rolls-Royce or Lamborghini passes by a group of strangers, half the onlookers seem jealous, the other half judgmental. We hate people who have what we want but can't seem to get. I guess insecurity is at the heart of it, but regardless of where it's coming from, we have to navigate it well. I have committed to prioritizing my friendships, which means, because of the fragile world we live in, I often have to prioritize the emotions of the people around me over my own desires. I'm not as frank with people in real life as I am in this book, because most wouldn't receive it well.

A few years ago, I was having dinner at my friends' home—let's call them "Johnny" and "Jackie." They are both successful real estate investors. As the night progressed, Jackie walked out of the room momentarily to feed their baby. Johnny and I were in the thick of it, sharing our lifelong dreams, when Jackie abruptly poked her head around the corner and asked, "Nate, has anyone ever told you that you're cocky?"

I had no idea where she was going with this, so I forced a smile and said, "All the time!"

They both erupted with laughter. Later on, they shared how their successes frequently strain their relationships. Their insatiable desires to strive for bigger and better dreams has caused people to view them as arrogant, greedy, or even self-centered. I know them well, and from my perspective, they're the furthest thing from any of these labels. They're incredibly kind, they mentor young men and women, and they serve their community better than most. Yet, they are misunderstood because they want more out of life.

As unfair as this is, I've experienced this firsthand, and I know many others who have voiced similar frustrations. In full transparency, writing this book has been challenging because honesty isn't always appreciated. I want to share what I believe to be true, but there's a voice in my head telling me people will be offended by my viewpoints. That's tough for me. I am very open to thoughts and opinions that contradict mine, but not everyone shares this same level of openness. People stuck in their ways might not be in a good place to read this book. My hope is that the right people will find this book and be bold enough to consider its message.

On the flip side, knowing I have to censor myself is helpful for my own growth. I want to build a relational environment where my friends feel free to show me my blind spots. Since I know the cost of not receiving corrections well, the last thing I want to do is keep myself from the blessing that this uncomfortable pruning can yield. I need the constructive criticism. I would be the same person, year after year, were it not for the books I read and the mentors who guide me.

Almost everything I've learned has come from someone else, whether from a book, a friend, or a mentor. These mentors have helped me get an edge in life. Even though I spend time with all kinds of people, my mentors are the ones who form my beliefs, raise my awareness, and shower me with wisdom. I need these people more than I need my job or any possession. My mentors are my biggest asset. When I find someone who's pure gold, I pursue friendship with them, even when it's not convenient. If they move away, I call them consistently. I send them encouraging texts. I do whatever it takes to keep them in my life.

What friendships will you cultivate to improve your life? What books will you read to expand your knowledge? Consider these questions carefully before moving on.

ACTION STEPS

1. WHO IS YOUR BUSINESS MENTOR? DO THEY FEEL EMPOWERED TO CALL YOU UP TO A HIGHER STANDARD?

_____

_____

_____

_____

2. WHO IS YOUR LIFE/SPIRITUAL MENTOR? DO THEY FEEL EMPOWERED TO CALL YOU UP TO A HIGHER STANDARD?

_____

_____

_____

_____

3. WHAT BOOKS SHOULD YOU READ NEXT?

_____

_____

_____

_____

> "
>
> You will be the same person in five years as you are today except for the people you meet and the books you read.
>
> **– CHARLIE TREMENDOUS JONES**

CHAPTER EIGHT

YOUR SUPERPOWER'S KRYPTONITE

Unfortunately, our superpowers are double-edged swords. Our greatest strengths are often our biggest Kryptonites. My biggest strengths are effectiveness, extreme single-tasking, and weapons-grade positivity. So, it's not much of a surprise that I struggle with workaholism and empathy for others. This double-edged sword phenomenon is evident in most gifted people, regardless of their personality type or particular superpower. Let me share a few stories to illustrate this principle.

When I immersed myself in the positivity cult, it was easy to believe they'd discovered the holy grail of living. Motivational speakers act like they've found the one truth that leads to happiness, wealth, and endless prosperity. If you follow them, you will be epic, and if you don't, you will end up a pathetic loser destined for a mediocre life. I'm exaggerating their stance a little, but that's roughly the gist of it.

Even though I have immensely benefited from the self-help way of thinking, there's a dark side to it. I first noticed this in one of my mentors—let's call this mentor "Bill." Bill is one of the most amazing humans I know; he has helped thousands of people reach their true potential because of his strong core beliefs he doesn't sway from.

I don't think running a high-performing company like Bill's would be possible without him consistently digging into his *why*. Bill uses positive self-talk and affirmations to overcome the negativity around him, employs regimented habits just like I do to get things done, and, in his own way, he is giving himself "an offer he can't refuse" regularly. So what's the problem? Isn't he doing everything I just advocated? Well, yes, but somewhere along the line, his company started encouraging unethical behaviors and publicly praising people for "getting out of their comfort zone" when they did something against their moral code. Anytime someone raised a concern, his leaders would praise blind followers all the more.

I'm almost positive this did not initiate with Bill. I don't think he had anything to do with it initially, but these little deceptions took root in his life because he believed in the end goal so wholeheartedly. Years of surrounding himself with yes-men made it easy for Bill to justify the unjustifiable. His superpower ended up being his Kryptonite.

Many young souls have tried to persuade Bill that the 90 percent good the company does doesn't excuse the shady 10 percent, but to no avail. Bill has inadvertently used affirmations and positive self-talk to silence the truth and convince himself that lying is okay because "it's all for the greater good." The Wolf of Wall Street did something similar, but he's only remembered for the crimes he committed, not all the positive things he did. Positive self-talk is a fantastic tool for silencing naysayers and negative thoughts, but it's dangerous when you use it to silence your conscience.

Here's a second example that's a little darker. I used to work for a business owner who, from the outside, appeared to be a great guy. He seemed to have it all figured out. He had a great business, a beautiful wife, and a couple of good-looking kids. However, under this perfect facade was an addictive lifestyle with insatiable appetites funded by consumer debt. He was a slave, not a champion. But most people didn't know it.

When I first went to work with him, I asked him specific metrics for the job and what I needed to achieve to make a certain income. He showed me compensation charts from his average employees, then from his top 1 percent of earners. Long story short, he grossly manipulated the figures he showed me. In my three years of working for him, no one in his entire organization hit his "average" numbers, let alone what he claimed the top 1 percent was earning. He was lying to us, but had no shame because he focused solely on positive things that fit his cookie-cutter worldview.

I gave him the benefit of the doubt for much longer than I should have, because sometimes we all say things we believe to be true but that don't end up being that way. I've accidentally done that myself. But that's not what I'm talking about here. The harsh reality was that his organization onboarded thousands of reps, and roughly 90 percent of them quit within their first two weeks. From there, attrition would systematically whack away at the employees until only approximately 2 percent of them remained a full year. And even that top 2 percent didn't make as much as he claimed was *average*.

It's been many years since I worked for him, but I still see his ads on Indeed and ZipRecruiter, boasting the same wildly inaccurate income statistics. He even changed his company name three times to avoid the backlash of his actions. But even with all the pushback, he keeps pressing forward. On the one hand, I admire his unrelenting perseverance amid obstacles, but on the other hand, what he's doing is plain wrong. He tells himself the same lies over and over and over; honestly, I think he believes them himself, despite the overwhelming evidence against them. It's tragic.

I have fully forgiven his misdeeds, for the record, so I'm not bringing this up to hold a grudge. The reason I am sharing this is that I want to give you a warning about the dark side of strong beliefs. Yes, they are extremely useful for overcoming impossible odds, which is why multi-level marketing companies and the military implement them; but when used for the wrong things, these motivational tactics can achieve staggering results for evil, instead of good. Consider yourself warned.

The same principle applies to my free-spirited friends on the complete opposite side of the personality spectrum. For many of my free-spirited friends whose superpower is human connection and emotional awareness, their Kryptonites might be things like inefficiency, procrastination, and lack of follow-through. They thrive on spending time with people, they love hanging out in coffee shops, but they struggle getting things done.

I know someone who is an almost supernaturally gifted singer. She sounds like Regina Spektor and has the songwriting chops to back it up. When she sings, you hear every little nuance of emotion as she glides from note to note. You feel happy, sad, joyful, and depressed all at once just hearing her sing. It takes people back to their childhood, and it's not uncommon to see people misty-eyed by the time she's done. She has an incredible gift, but like I mentioned, every superpower has its Kryptonite; every gift has its curse.

I hadn't seen her in a few years, but she recently sang at a wedding I attended. I was blown away, instantly reminded of how incredibly talented she is. In my mind, she's the kind of person who should be world-renowned for her art—but unfortunately, hardly anyone has heard of her.

Her Kryptonite is that she lacks follow-through. She sings when she wants to and doesn't push herself to make things happen. Even though I know she's gifted, no one else does, because there's virtually no way to find her. She hasn't recorded any of her music, so you can't find her on places like Spotify, and she doesn't perform on live stages very often, so you won't stumble across her there, either. She doesn't have any exposure, so her talent remains stagnant.

If she pushed herself to create her art consistently and then convinced capable marketers to help her, I feel confident she would have been a household name by now. Instead, she settled for an average life with a mind-numbing job and sings in her free time. This makes me sad. So many people would kill to have her gift, yet her talents have been squandered. If she could face her Kryptonite, she could live a much more exciting life.

But on the other hand, who am I to judge? There's a possibility she could have pursued greatness with her gift and ended up a sad junky like Amy Winehouse. In that case, a boring life would have been preferable. That's one of the great ironies of life; so often, the decisions we make with the greatest of intentions end up giving us the exact opposite of what we wanted. The people who say, "Oh, I don't want to be like those money-hungry people. They're greedy. All they focus on is money," are the same people who spend their lives stressed about money. The people who say, "I just want an easy job so I can live my life," end up slaving away at dead-end jobs the rest of their lives—which is, arguably, much harder than the life they were intent on avoiding. The people who say they're too tired to get up and go to the gym end up being more lethargic because of it. Life is funny that way.

And believe me, I am not immune to this. My natural tendency is to work so hard I destroy the very things I'm working for. I tell myself I'm working for my wife and future kids, and then I'm so focused on work that I accidentally neglect our relationship. I tell myself I'm building an empire to fund missionaries and charity organizations, but end up so focused on that one target that I forget to love the homeless guy on the corner. We all miss it at some point, but there's power in recognizing when we are missing it. Superman's Kryptonite was a physical element that was easy to identify. Our Kryptonites are much harder to recognize. They are ever-evolving and ever-changing, hiding behind legitimate needs and desires but overtaking that which is most significant. Just like an invasive weed, it chokes the lifeblood out of us.

My journey started with crushing fear and indecision, which led me to significantly better results. From there, achievements themselves became the Kryptonite I needed to crush because they turned into the very thing keeping me from loving the people around me. Trying to love people well turned into unhealthy people-pleasing, which led to me becoming an ineffective blob of Jell-O. And the cycle continues.

So the question is, how do you neutralize the dark side of your superpower? How do you face your Kryptonites, knowing there's a strong possibility overcoming one Kryptonite will just create a new one? I don't have a perfect answer for you, but I do have some thoughts that have been helpful in my life.

I have found that being friends with and having mentors who have various strengths and weaknesses is very helpful. Self-awareness is a key component, and self-awareness is significantly aided by surrounding yourself with a community that will help you see your blind spots. We all have blind spots. There's no shame in that, but we do need to expose and address our blind spots as we pursue wholeness.

CHAPTER NINE

HOW WILL *YOU* CRUSH YOUR KRYPTONITE?

Do any of the Kryptonites discussed so far sound familiar? Have you failed to recognize them in your life until now? Don't worry—here's the chapter that will teach you how to get out of your own way and really crush your Kryptonite.

First, let me tell you a story about a life-changing moment. In 2018, I moved to the suburbs of Dallas to figure out what my next chess move in life would be. I interviewed with over twenty companies, most of which were not a good fit on my end; the one company I did want to work for only had opportunities for me in other states. I felt like a single girl at prom.

Somewhere in the monotony of going nowhere, a seed of doubt sprouted inside me. What if I'm the problem? What if I'm perpetually stuck? Were my last couple career moves mistakes? The future seemed bleak. The more I struck out, the more I got in my own head. So I tried a new strategy. Instead of chasing open positions, I would find a unique way to find work. The challenge with job postings is that thousands of people comb through them every day. This inundates the interviewers with an endless amount of potential candidates, to the point where everyone starts to look the same. On the other side, companies do the same thing. Every company does its best to impress potential hires. They all say roughly the same things, so as a hopeful employee it is easy to get lost in a similar ambiguity after a while.

Overwhelm and fatigue were setting in, so I faced my fear and forced myself to meet new people. I started making Uber runs in downtown Dallas, around the times of day when I was most likely to drive business professionals. I chauffeured hundreds of upper-class business people who were too focused and busy to drive themselves. When possible, I made a point to ask them what they did for a living. These conversations got me a few job interviews, but I still didn't find the right fit.

I was making progress, but it was so slow that fatigue set in once again. The epiphany came when I drove one particular individual twice in the same week. He had long blond hair, looked like he was fresh out of Cali, and wore the same suit both times I saw him. He was a carefree, jolly individual and was enjoyable to be around, but I soon realized through our conversations that he was a smiling schmuck. I'm not trying to be mean, but I'm mentioning this because it seems unlikely he had put himself through a tenth of the hardships and professional growth I had. He hadn't taken the hits I had. He hadn't been kicked in the teeth before. He was just a cool dude living out his best life. How had this guy beat me to the six-figure club? I don't even think he tried! This was his first job ever, and he was already winning.

My takeaway from this event was that he beat me because he was naive enough not to realize the ceiling he had busted through. My belief level had been keeping me down. I was questioning my worth. If I wanted a high-level position, I couldn't show up to an interview like a regular person. I would have to show up believing that I was special, like that guy did. I would have to show up convinced I was different and that I was the best fit for them.

The universe doesn't limit us. We limit us. We look at the mountain ahead and decide it will be a monumental task to climb before we even start. It's like we're an actor choosing to play the role of a character who is incapable of getting what they want. Once we've trained ourselves to play that role, it's hard to pick another one. This is where the hard work of self-talk comes in. The hard work isn't climbing the mountain itself; it's convincing yourself that you're worthy and capable of climbing the mountain. You must brainwash yourself into believing you're a champion before anyone else will acknowledge that in you. That's the real battle.

So that brings us to the critical question: what is your Kryptonite? What is currently bleeding you dry? What is the thorn in your side that you have allowed to exist? What is keeping you from your dreams?

I don't know the answer, but you do. You know exactly what's been holding you back.

If you picked up this book, it's most likely because you aren't satisfied with some area in your life. Even if you're reading this book by accident, statistically speaking, I'm sure you aren't content with some area of your life. If you don't crush it, it will continue crushing you.

The follow-up question is: are you angry enough at the problem that you're willing to deal with it? Are you prepared to incinerate it? Eviscerate it? Destroy, mar, and maim it? If there's a righteous anger brewing within you, are you finally ready to do something about it?

I hope you are, because life is far too precious to accept *average* when you were created for *greatness*.

Get Clarity and Commit to Destroying Your Kryptonite

Taking the first step to crush your Kryptonite is always the hardest, so I want to give you an actionable plan to follow.

The first step is to get clarity. For many people, perpetual noise cripples their brainpower before they ever get a chance to face their biggest Kryptonite. After they've wasted their energy on meaningless "busyness" and entertainment, they don't have the resolve to improve difficult situations. Does that sound like you?

It's nearly impossible to achieve greatness when you're filling your life with chaos and perpetual noise, so cut it out of your life. Create margin in your day and give your brain the space to think. Please, take the time right now to pause reading this book so you can quiet your mind and identify your biggest Kryptonite.

The second step is to commit. Take the knowledge you have gained by reading this book and commit to brutally destroying your Kryptonite. Deal with it now, so you don't have to deal with it later.

The third step is to establish a positive self-improvement routine. Consistent habits are vital to systematically obliterating your Kryptonites. I want to throw in a plug for *The Miracle Morning* by Hal Elrod. It has made a fundamental difference in speeding up growth in my life, and I believe it can help you too. *The Miracle Morning* taught me to invest the first hour of my day in myself.

My current morning routine is as follows:

- 5-10 minutes of meditation (meditation music on Spotify helps)
- 20 minutes of self-improvement books (Audible is a great way to do this)
- 20 minutes reading the Bible
- 10 minutes of gratitude (writing down things I'm thankful for)

I finish it with a quick home-fitness regimen or a quick 30 minutes at the gym.

Create your morning routine any way you like, but keep in mind that consistency is the key to winning at anything. You will feel incredible and in control of your life once you start building yourself consistently. To take care of your boss, clients, and significant other, you must take care of yourself, first. Aggressive self-care should be a priority as you endeavor to crush your Kryptonite. By being in tune with yourself and committing to growth, you will automatically find weaknesses to crush and superpowers to improve.

The fourth step is to surround yourself with mentors who make you better. Robert Kiyosaki was the first self-help author I was introduced to, at the age of five or six when my father read his book *Rich Dad, Poor Dad*. One of Kiyosaki's mottos I have claimed as my own is, "choose your teacher." I want to encourage you to follow his advice. Learn from the best when pursuing greatness and for the critical areas of life, only take advice from someone you would gladly trade places with. If you want to be healthy, learn from the healthiest people. If you want financial literacy, learn from the wealthiest people. If you're going to grow in empathy and kindness—you guessed it—surround yourself with the kindest people. And for the love of all things good and beautiful, please *don't* get all your business advice from a tenured professor who hasn't run a successful business before. You can learn from anything and anyone, but you have to choose your mentors wisely, so take counsel from those who are winning at life.

A great source of "mentor" wisdom is books like this one. The average Fortune 500 CEO reads fifty-two books a year, while their average employee only reads one.[5] Who do you want to be? The CEO or the employee? Through the power of books, you can learn from people like Michael Jordan's coach, Grant Cardone, Simon Sinek, or anyone else who has mastery in an area you want to grow in. We are blessed to live in the information age, where all the world's knowledge is at our fingertips. Take advantage of it.

The final step is to take action. A stranger once told me that education is the most socially acceptable form of procrastination. I couldn't agree more. Knowledge is useless until it is put to use. We all know people who spend so much time accumulating knowledge, listening to podcasts,

---

[5] Evans, B. D. (2017, June 27). *Most CEOS read a book a week. this is how you can too (according to this renowned brain coach)*. Inc.com. Retrieved January 18, 2022, from https://www.inc.com/brian-d-evans/most-ceos-read-a-book-a-week-this-is-how-you-can-too-according-to-this-renowned-.html

and watching TEDTalks that they end up paralyzing themselves and never do any of it. They devour motivational content and repeat it ad nauseam to their friends, but when they regurgitate their sound-bites of wisdom, it rings hollow because they haven't ever used those pieces of advice themselves. Analysis paralysis is not healthy. Education should lead to understanding, which should always lead to action; otherwise, consuming knowledge is pointless.

You now have the knowledge you need to overcome your weakness and unleash your superpower. Now it's time to put it to use. I hope this book has inspired you and given you the confidence you need to take massive action in your life and to Crush Your Kryptonite!

FINAL ACTION STEPS

1. BUILD YOUR CONFIDENCE BY WRITING THREE PAST INSTANCES WHERE YOU CRUSHED YOUR KRYPTONITE.

2. WHAT IS THE #1 KRYPTONITE YOU NEED TO CRUSH?

3. HOW WILL YOU CRUSH IT?

> "
> The secret of getting ahead
> is getting started.
>
> – **MARK TWAIN**

BOOKS TO READ
FOR FURTHER DEVELOPMENT

BOOKS ON HAPPINESS:

BOOKS TO GROW YOUR EFFECTIVENESS:

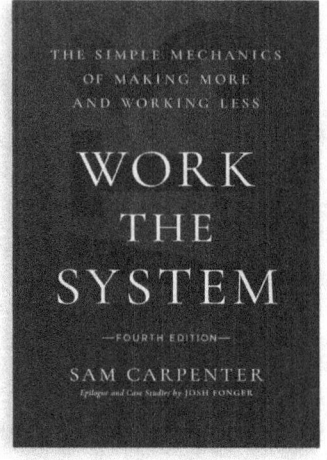

BOOKS ABOUT FOCUS:

Self-Publishing School helped me, and now I want to help you with this FREE resource to begin writing your book!

Even if you're busy, bad at writing, or don't know where to start, you CAN write a bestseller and build your best life.

With tools and experience across a variety of niches and professions, Self-Publishing School is the only resource you need to take your book to the finish line!

Self-publishingschool.com/friend

Follow the steps on the page to get a FREE resource to get started on your book and unlock a discount to get started with Self-Publishing School!

URGENT PLEA!

Thank You For Reading My Book!

I really appreciate all of your feedback and
I love hearing what you have to say.

I need your input to make the next version of this
book and my future books better.

Please take two minutes now to leave a helpful review on
Amazon letting me know what you thought of the book:

crushyourkryptonite.com/review

Thanks so much!

– Nate Hambrick

www.ingramcontent.com/pod-product-compliance
Lightning Source LLC
Chambersburg PA
CBHW070743060526
44119CB00092B/425/J